vegetarian

Baked veggie salad, p. 38

Kasha soup with wild mushrooms, p. 70

Polenta with mushrooms, p. 132

Farfalle with yogurt & avocado p. 144

Stuffed potato croquettes, p. 192

Vegetarian curry with brow rice, p. 228

Bell peppers with mushroom couscous, p. 238

Macedonian spinach pie, p. 300

Filled focaccia with gorgonzo & bell peppers, p. 310

MICHELA NERI

vegetarian

DELICIOUS RECIPES FOR A HEALTHY LIFE

This book was conceived, edited and designed
by McRae Publishing Ltd, London
info@mcraebooks.com
www.mcraepublishing.co.uk
Publishers Anne McRae, Marco Nardi

Project Director Anne McRae
Art Director Marco Nardi
Photography Brent Parker Jones
Text Michela Neri
Editing Foreign Concept
Food Styling Lee Blaylock
Layouts Filippo Delle Monache

NOTE TO OUR READERS
Eating eggs or egg whites that are not completely cooked poses the possibility of salmonella food poisoning. The risk is greater for pregnant women, the elderly, the very young, and persons with impaired immune systems. If you are concerned about salmonella, you can use reconstituted powdered egg whites or pasteurized eggs.

ISBN 978-1-910122-21-1
Printed in China

Contents

Introduction

People follow vegetarian diets for a wide variety of reasons, including the desire for better health, a safer and cleaner environment, a more ethical treatment of animals, and a fairer division of the Earth's dwindling resources. Vegetarians are equally diverse in the ways they follow their plant-based diets. The strictest vegetarians, called vegans, enjoy fruits, vegetables, whole grains and cereals, legumes, seeds, and nuts, but they exclude all animal products, including dairy, eggs, and honey. However, the majority of vegetarians include some dairy, eggs, and honey in their diets. There is also another, rapidly growing group of people who are not strict vegetarians because they still eat some fish and chicken, or even small amounts of red meat. Most of these "flexitarians" would prefer not to eat meat at all but for practical reasons have not entirely eliminated it. This book, with its wealth of simple and delicious recipes, will be especially useful for them since it makes following a vegetarian diet so easy.

Here you will find more than 140 recipes for a wide range of vegetarian dishes, from soups and salads to pasta, rice, egg, tofu, and vegetable dishes. With this book you can prepare gourmet vegetarian meals every day of the week. Enjoy!

SYMBOLS		Serves 4–6	**Serves** The number of portions
		30 minutes	**Preparation** Time to prepare the dish, excluding cooking & resting
		1 hour	**Chilling & Resting** "Down time" when dish is chilling, resting, etc
These symbols are used throughout the book. They mean:		15 minutes	**Cooking** Cooking time
		2	**Difficulty** From 1 (easy) to 3 (challenging). Most recipes are 1 or 2

opposite: pumpkin & lentil tagine, p. 222

choosing a dish

This book has more than 140 recipes for delicious vegetarian dishes—something for everyone, and every occasion. But what if you are not an experienced cook or are looking for something exotic? The EASY section below will help with the first problem and the INTERNATIONAL CUISINES on page 14 will solve the second. Looking for an old favorite? See our CLASSICS suggestions. See also the QUICK, CHALLENGING, DETOX, and EDITOR'S CHOICE recommendations.

EASY

cumin rice with tomatoes, p. 112

spicy pumpkin & chili soup, p. 60

raw energy salad, p. 30

fusilli with mushrooms
p. 140

grilled summer vegetables,
p. 178

leek tartlets,
p. 288

potato cakes with cherry tomatoes, p. 252

spiced couscous with mushrooms, p. 104

rigatoni with cauliflower, p. 138

stir-fried vegetables with noodles, p. 206

fiery eggs with cherry tomatoes, p. 268

cucumber, radish & goat cheese salad p. 26

CHALLENGING

watercress tagliolini with pesto, p. 158

fresh pasta with scallions & tomatoes, p. 156

tomato croquettes p. 200

vegetable samosas, p. 202

savory bake p. 244

aromatic lemon rice, p. 114

pad thai, p. 208

pineapple curry with coconut, p. 230

spicy tofu, p. 280

nasi goreng, p. 126

DETOX

green bean & zucchini ratatouille p. 220

fruit & nut quinoa salad, p. 44

chilled zucchini & yogurt soup p. 52

vegetarian curry with brown rice, p. 228

tofu & black bean stir-fry, p. 278

falafel with tabbouleh p. 100

portuguese caldo verde
p. 66

vegetarian paella, p. 124

caponata with rice, p. 212

focaccia with sage
& olives, p. 302

EDITOR'S CHOICE

spiced tomato soup, p. 76

risotto with red roses,
p. 122

pasta salad with feta & olives, p. 48

pan-fried potatoes with
sun-dried tomatoes, p. 186

red bean chili, p. 224

basil frittata, p. 272

herb & tomato focaccia,
p. 306

salads

spinach salad
with orange & avocado

This salad makes a delicious and healthy starter or light lunch. Serve with freshly baked whole-grain bread.

🍽 Serves 4–6

⏱ 15 minutes

🍴 1

2	large ripe oranges
8	ounces (250 g) baby spinach leaves
2	large ripe avocados, peeled, pitted, and sliced
	Freshly squeezed juice of 1 lemon
¼	cup (60 ml) extra-virgin olive oil

2	scallions (spring onions), trimmed and sliced
	Finely grated zest of 1 unwaxed orange
	Salt and freshly ground black pepper

1. **Peel** the oranges using a sharp knife, removing all the bitter white pith. Break the fruit into segments.

2. **Put** the spinach leaves in a large salad bowl. Top with the oranges and avocados.

3. **Beat** the lemon juice and oil in a small bowl with a fork.

4. **Add** the scallions and orange zest and season with salt and pepper. Beat well.

5. **Drizzle** the dressing over the salad and toss carefully.

6. **Serve** at once.

If you liked this recipe, you will love these as well.

orange & watercress salad

20

spinach & fennel salad with strawberries & almonds

22

cheese salad with fresh fruit & herbs

24

orange & watercress salad

Watercress is a very healthy food and was used as a healing herb by the ancient Greeks. Modern science has proved them right, identifying more than 15 essential vitamins and minerals in this tasty salad green. Watercress has more iron than spinach, more calcium than milk, and more vitamin C than oranges.

◉ Serves 4

🕐 10 minutes

🍳 1–2 minutes

🍸 1

SALAD

2	cups (100 g) watercress
2	large oranges
3	carrots, grated
1	head green or red radicchio, torn
2	tablespoons fresh pomegranate seeds
1	tablespoon sunflower seeds
1	tablespoon pumpkin seeds

DRESSING

2	tablespoons freshly squeezed lemon juice
1	tablespoon pomegranate juice (from the seeds)
1	teaspoon Dijon mustard
1/4	cup (60 ml) grapeseed oil or sunflower oil
	Salt and freshly ground black pepper

1. **Put** the watercress in a salad bowl. Grate the orange zest and set aside.

2. **Peel** the oranges and pare off the white pith. Cut the flesh crosswise into thin slices, removing any seeds, and add to the bowl. Add the carrots and radicchio.

3. **Open** the pomegranate, cut into sections, and remove the seeds. Carefully discard the bitter pith and add most of the seeds to the bowl, reserving a few for juicing.

4. **Toast** the sunflower and pumpkin seeds in a pan over high heat until nutty, 1–2 minutes.

5. **Combine** the lemon juice, pomegranate juice, and mustard in a screw-top jar. Add the orange zest and oil. Season with salt and pepper. Cover and shake well.

6. **Drizzle** over the salad and toss. Garnish with the seeds and serve.

If you liked this recipe, you will love these as well.

spinach salad with orange & avocado

18

spinach & fennel salad with strawberries & almonds

22

cheese salad with fresh fruit & herbs

24

spinach & fennel salad
with strawberries & almonds

This attractive salad can be served either as an appetizer or a light meal. Choose locally grown, organic strawberries and use the best quality balsamic vinegar you can afford. Divine!

Serves 4

15 minutes

5 minutes

1

SALAD

⅔	cup (100 g) blanched almonds
12	ounces (350 g) baby spinach leaves
12	ounces (350 g) strawberries, sliced
1	fennel bulb, thinly sliced

DRESSING

	Freshly squeezed juice of ½ lemon
	Freshly squeezed juice of 1 orange
¼	cup (60 ml) extra-virgin olive oil
2	tablespoons balsamic vinegar
1	teaspoon Dijon mustard
	Salt and freshly ground black pepper

1. **To prepare the salad,** toast the almonds in a large frying pan over medium heat until golden brown, about 5 minutes. Remove from the heat and let cool. Combine the spinach, strawberries, fennel, and almonds in a large salad bowl. Toss gently.

2. **To prepare the dressing,** beat the lemon juice, orange juice, oil, vinegar, and mustard in a small bowl with a fork. Season with salt and pepper.

3. **Drizzle** the dressing over the salad and toss gently. Serve immediately.

If you liked this recipe, you will love these as well.

spinach salad with orange & avocado

18

orange & watercress salad

20

cheese salad with fresh fruit & herbs

24

cheese salad
with fresh fruit & herbs

You can vary the cheese in this salad according to what you like or have on hand. Any tasty semi-firm or firm table cheese will work well.

 Serves 6

20 minutes

1

4	ounces (120 g) Emmental (Swiss) cheese, diced
4	ounces (120 g) Parmesan cheese, in flakes
1	small radicchio, torn
1	head frisée (curly endive), chopped
1	apple, peeled, cored, and diced
1	pear, peeled, cored, and diced
½	cup (75 g) green grapes, halved
2	tablespoons golden raisins (sultanas)
1	orange, peeled and cut in segments
1	grapefruit, peeled and cut in segments
1	shallot, finely chopped
¼	cup (60 ml) extra-virgin olive oil
1	tablespoon balsamic vinegar
1	tablespoon whole-grain mustard
2	tablespoons each finely chopped fresh dill, chives, parsley
	Salt and freshly ground white pepper

1. **Combine** both cheeses in a large salad bowl.

2. **Add** the radicchio, frisée, apple, pear, grapes, golden raisins, orange, grapefruit, and shallot. Toss well.

3. **Beat** the oil and vinegar in a small bowl with a fork. Add the mustard, dill, chives, and parsley. Season with salt and white pepper and beat again.

4. **Drizzle** the salad with the dressing and toss gently.

5. **Serve** at once.

If you liked this recipe, you will love these as well.

spinach salad with orange & avocado

18

orange & watercress salad

20

spinach & fennel salad with strawberries & almonds

22

cucumber, radish & goat cheese salad

Be sure to have plenty of freshly baked, crusty bread on hand to serve with this salad.

Serves 4

15 minutes

1

DRESSING

- ⅓ cup (90 ml) heavy (double) cream
- ¼ cup (60 ml) plain nonfat yogurt
- 3 tablespoons finely chopped fresh mint leaves + 3–4 mint leaves to garnish
- 1 tablespoon finely chopped fresh parsley
- 1 teaspoon freshly squeezed lemon juice
  Salt and freshly ground white pepper

SALAD

- 1 medium cucumber
- 12 radishes, trimmed
- ½ red onion, peeled
  Handful of fresh mint leaves
- ¼ cup fresh parsley leaves
- ⅓ cup (100 g) crumbled soft fresh goat cheese
- 3 tablespoons extra-virgin olive oil
- 1 tablespoon red wine vinegar
  Crusty, freshly baked bread, to serve

1. **To prepare the dressing,** combine the cream, yogurt, chopped mint, and parsley in a bowl and whisk well. Add the lemon juice, salt, and white pepper. Transfer to a small serving bowl, garnish with mint leaves, and chill until needed.

2. **To prepare the salad,** peel the cucumber lightly, to remove the coarse skin only, leaving as much green as possible. Cut in half lengthwise and scrape out the seeds with a teaspoon. Halve each half lengthwise again, and cut into 1½-inch (4-cm) pieces. Put into a large salad bowl.

3. **Slice** the radishes to a thickness of ¼ inch (5 mm) or thinner, or cut into 6 wedges, and add to the cucumber.

4. **Slice** the onion thinly and separate into rings. Add to the bowl.

5. **Tear** the mint leaves into the bowl. Mix in the parsley leaves and the cheese.

6. **Drizzle** with oil and vinegar, and top with freshly ground black pepper. Mix everything together.

7. **Serve** the salad with crusty, freshly baked bread and pass the dressing in a bowl on the side for everybody to help themselves.

dandelion & garden flowers
with quail eggs

Don't use any leaves or flowers that have been sprayed with chemicals. You could also use honeysuckle flowers, marsh marigolds (cowslip), primrose, pansies, or violets. If you can't get quail eggs, use four ordinary hard-boiled hen's eggs.

Serves 4

15 minutes

2 minutes

1

8	quail eggs	
1	cup (50 g) arugula (rocket) or lamb's lettuce	
1	cup (50 g) young dandelion leaves, torn	
	Handful of red radicchio or purple basil	
20	borage flowers	
1	rose, petals only	
1/2	cup (25 g) arugula	
15	nasturtiums	
1	tablespoon fresh dill	

Marigold petals

Zest of 1 lemon, finely chopped

2 tablespoons freshly grated Parmesan

Salt and freshly ground black pepper

Freshly squeezed juice of 1/2 lemon

3 tablespoons grapeseed oil

1. **Put** the quail eggs in a saucepan, cover with cold water, and boil for 2 minutes. Refresh in cold water and set aside.

2. **Put** all the leaves and flowers in a shallow glass bowl. Sprinkle with the lemon zest and Parmesan, and season with salt and pepper. Drizzle with the lemon juice and grapeseed oil and lightly toss with your fingers.

3. **Top** with the eggs, and serve.

If you liked this recipe, you will love these as well.

cucumber, radish & goat cheese salad
26

raw energy salad
30

three-bean salad with fresh asparagus
36

raw energy salad

This salad is packed with goodness and hearty, nourishing ingredients. It makes a perfect pick-me-up after a work out at the gym.

 Serves 4

15 minutes

3–5 minutes

1

SALAD

¼	cup (45 g) pumpkin seeds
¼	cup (45 g) sunflower seeds
2	tablespoons sesame seeds
2	teaspoons cumin seeds
¼	red cabbage, finely shredded
1	large carrot, grated
1	cooked beet (beetroot), grated
2	cups (100 g) baby spinach leaves, finely chopped
1	red onion, thinly sliced
¼	cup (45 g) dried currants
3	tablespoons finely chopped fresh mint

DRESSING

	Finely grated zest and juice of 1 orange
3	tablespoons pomegranate molasses
1	tablespoon extra-virgin olive oil
	Salt and freshly ground black pepper

1. **To prepare the salad,** toast the pumpkin, sunflower, sesame, and cumin seeds in a medium frying pan over medium heat until golden brown, 3–5 minutes.

2. **Combine** the red cabbage, carrot, beet, spinach, onion, currants, mint, and toasted seeds in a large salad bowl.

3. **To prepare the dressing,** whisk the orange zest and juice, pomegranate molasses, and oil in a small bowl. Pour over the salad and toss to combine. Season with salt and pepper and serve.

If you liked this recipe, you will love these as well.

orange & watercress salad
20

cucumber, radish & goat cheese salad
26

dandelion & garden flowers with quail eggs
28

grilled summer salad

This makes a healthy and nourishing lunch dish. Serve with plenty of freshly baked whole-wheat (wholemeal) or multigrain bread for a complete meal.

Serves 6

35 minutes

15–20 minutes

2

SALAD

8	ounces (250 g) mozzarella cheese, cut into ½-inch (1-cm) slices
8	tablespoons (120 ml) extra-virgin olive oil + extra to drizzle
1	clove garlic, finely chopped
	Salt and freshly ground black pepper
	Dash of Tabasco
2	tablespoons finely chopped fresh basil
1	teaspoon finely grated lemon zest
2	red bell peppers (capsicums), halved
1	yellow bell pepper (capsicum), halved
1	eggplant (aubergine), cut lengthwise into ¼-inch (5-mm) slices
5	zucchini (courgettes), cut lengthwise into ¼-inch (5-mm) slices
1	fennel bulb, trimmed, cut into ¼-inch (5-mm) slices
4	plum tomatoes, cut into ½-inch (1-cm) slices

DRESSING

⅓	cup (90 ml) extra-virgin olive oil
2	tablespoons balsamic vinegar
2	scallions (spring onions), trimmed and thinly sliced
¼	cup fresh basil

1. **To prepare the salad,** put the mozzarella on a plate. Mix 2 tablespoons of oil with the garlic, salt, pepper, and Tabasco in a bowl. Drizzle over the mozzarella and sprinkle with half the basil and lemon zest. Set aside while you prepare the vegetables.

2. **Cook** the bell peppers skin side up, under a hot broiler (grill) until blackened. Place in a plastic bag and let cool. Remove the skins, core, and seeds. Cut into quarters lengthwise.

3. **Preheat** a grill pan (griddle) for 5 minutes, or use a very hot broiler (grill). Pour the remaining 6 tablespoons of oil into a large shallow dish. Dip the eggplant, coating both sides. Grill until browned, then turn over and cook the other side. They are done when soft and crisscrossed with grill marks.

4. **Transfer** to a plate, and season with salt and pepper. Repeat with the zucchini and fennel.

5. **Drizzle** the tomatoes with oil. Grill on both sides, until softened, 1–2 minutes. Transfer to a plate and season with salt and the remaining basil.

6. **Arrange** the cheese and vegetables attractively in a wide salad bowl.

7. **To prepare the dressing,** whisk the oil and vinegar in a bowl. Stir in the scallions and season with salt and pepper.

8. **Drizzle** the dressing over the vegetables.

9. **Add** a squeeze of lemon juice and some pepper, and sprinkle with the basil.

lentil & herb salad

Small green Le Puy lentils come from Le Puy in France. They are perfect for salads as they hold their shape during cooking and don't become mushy.

Serves 4

10 minutes

15 minutes

25–30 minutes

1

¾ cup (150 g) Le Puy lentils
1 clove garlic, peeled
3 tablespoons finely chopped fresh parsley
3 tablespoons finely chopped fresh basil
2 tablespoons finely chopped fresh arugula (rocket)
1 cup (50 g) watercress, thick stems discarded

¼ cup (60 ml) extra-virgin olive oil, + extra to drizzle
1 tablespoon sherry or red wine vinegar
Salt and freshly ground black pepper
½ cup (60 g) pecorino cheese, shaved
2 lemons, cut into wedges, to serve

1. **Rinse** the lentils under running cold water. Place in a saucepan, cover with cold water about 1 inch (2.5 cm) above the level of the lentils, and add the garlic. Bring to a boil, then turn down the heat and simmer until tender, 25–30 minutes. Drain well and set aside to cool for 15 minutes.

2. **Meanwhile**, chop half the watercress and add to the other fresh herbs. Drain the lentils and remove the garlic. Stir in the oil and vinegar and season with salt.

3. **Add** the herbs to the lentils while they are still warm and toss well.

4. **Mix** the remaining watercress leaves and pecorino into the salad.

5. **Divide** among individual salad bowls or arrange on a large serving plate, making sure you don't break up the fragile cheese shavings.

6. **Drizzle** with a little extra oil and serve with the lemon wedges.

If you liked this recipe, you will love these as well.

raw energy salad
30

three-bean salad with fresh asparagus
36

pumpkin & lentil tagine
222

three-bean salad
with fresh asparagus

This healthy salad makes a complete meal in itself. Serve with freshly baked bread to soak up the extra dressing.

- Serves 4–6
- 30 minutes
- 13–17 minutes
- 1

SALAD

1	pound (500 g) fava (broad) beans in shells, or 8 ounces (250 g) frozen beans
8	ounces (250 g) green beans, trimmed
5	ounces (150 g) snow peas (mangetout), trimmed
16	green asparagus spears, trimmed
1	(14-ounce/400-g) can borlotti or red kidney beans, drained
15	black olives, pitted
8	ounces (250 g) feta or mozzarella cheese, cut into small cubes
5	fresh basil leaves, torn

DRESSING

¼	cup fresh basil
2	tablespoons white wine vinegar
⅓	cup (90 ml) extra-virgin olive oil
1	clove garlic, peeled
	Salt and freshly ground black pepper

1. **To prepare the salad,** put the fava beans in a pan of unsalted boiling water and simmer for 3–4 minutes. Drain, refresh in cold water, and peel off their tough outer skins. If using frozen beans, cook according to instructions on the package. Set aside.

2. **Cook** the green beans in a medium pan of salted boiling water until crunchy tender, 4–6 minutes. Drain, rinse in cold water, and set aside.

3. **Cook** the snow peas in a small pan of salted boiling water for 2 minutes. Drain, rinse under cold water, and set aside.

4. **Blanch** the asparagus spears in salted boiling water until just tender, 4–5 minutes. Drain and let cool.

5. **Chop** the basil, vinegar, oil, garlic, salt, and pepper in a blender. Transfer to a small bowl.

6. **Combine** the vegetables, borlotti or red kidney beans, olives, and cheese in a salad bowl. Drizzle with the dressing.

7. **Toss** lightly. Sprinkle with the basil, and serve.

If you liked this recipe, you will love these as well.

raw energy salad

30

lentil & herb salad

34

fruit & nut quinoa salad

44

baked veggie salad

This hearty salad is perfect during the cold winter months. You can vary the vegetables according to what you have in the pantry or refrigerator.

Serves 4–6

30 minutes

45–50 minutes

2

SALAD

3	parsnips, peeled
6	medium potatoes, scrubbed clean
1	sweet potato, about 12 ounces (350 g), scrubbed clean
4	cloves garlic, peeled
1	teaspoon salt
¼	cup (60 ml) canola (rapeseed) oil or extra-virgin olive oil
10	cherry tomatoes, halved
2	ripe pears
1	cup (50 g) arugula (rocket)

DRESSING

⅓	cup (90 ml) freshly squeezed orange juice + extra to drizzle
2	teaspoons balsamic vinegar
2	tablespoons extra-virgin olive oil
1	scant tablespoon honey
3	sprigs fresh rosemary, leaves only
	Salt and freshly ground black pepper
2	tablespoons pine nuts, toasted, to garnish

1. **To prepare the salad,** cut the parsnips lengthwise into halves or quarters, depending on size, and then into 2-inch (5-cm) pieces.

2. **Keep** the skin on the potatoes and cut them into 6 wedges. Top and tail the sweet potato, keep the skin on, and halve it widthwise. Cut each half into 3–4 wedges.

3. **Preheat** the oven to 350°F (180°C/gas 4). Combine the parsnips, potato, sweet potato, and garlic in a large roasting pan. Sprinkle with the salt and drizzle with the oil. Mix well, coating in the oil.

4. **Roast** for 35–40 minutes, until the vegetables are golden, crisp on the outside, and soft inside.

5. **To prepare the dressing,** whisk the orange juice with the vinegar, oil, and honey in a bowl.

6. **Finely** chop the rosemary and add to the dressing. Season with salt and pepper. Remove the roasting pan from the oven and drizzle half the dressing over the vegetables.

7. **Add** the tomatoes and return to the oven. Roast for another 10 minutes.

8. **Peel,** core, and slice the pears into 6–8 pieces. Mix with the arugula in a bowl and toss with the remaining dressing. Transfer the roasted vegetables with their juices to a large bowl. Top with the pears and arugula, and toss gently.

9. **Arrange** the salad on individual salad plates or in a large serving dish. Sprinkle with the pine nuts, and serve.

pesto potato salad

The fresh pesto in this salad is a real treat and melds beautifully with the potatoes.

 Serves 6

⏱ 30 minutes

🍳 20–25 minutes

🍴 2

SALAD
3	large eggs
1¾	pounds (800 g) small waxy salad potatoes, scrubbed
2	tablespoons capers
2	tablespoons finely chopped fresh parsley leaves
1	tablespoon freshly squeezed lemon juice
1	tablespoon warm water (optional)
	Salt and freshly ground black pepper

PESTO
1	cup (50 g) fresh parsley leaves
½	cup (25 g) watercress leaves
1	large clove garlic
	Salt
¼	cup (30 g) freshly grated Parmesan
⅓	cup (60 g) pine nuts
⅔	cup (150 ml) extra-virgin olive oil

1. **To prepare the salad,** put the eggs in a saucepan, cover with cold water, and boil for 5 minutes. Refresh in cold water, peel, and set aside.

2. **Cover** the potatoes in a medium pan with cold water, bring to a boil, and cook until tender, 12–18 minutes. Drain well and let cool a little.

3. **Cut** the potatoes in cubes and put them into a salad bowl.

4. **To prepare the pesto,** chop the parsley, watercress, garlic, cheese, and pine nuts in a food processor and chop until smooth. Slowly add the oil and pulse until you have a runny paste.

5. **Pour** the pesto over the potatoes. Stir in the capers, half the parsley, and lemon juice. Add the water if the potatoes are too dry. Season with salt and plenty of pepper.

6. **Coarsely** chop the eggs and gently mix into the salad. Garnish with the remaining parsley.

7. **Serve** warm or at room temperature.

If you liked this recipe, you will love these as well.

baked veggie salad

38

fruit & nut quinoa salad

44

potato cakes with cherry tomatoes

252

vegetarian salade niçoise

This recipe is a vegetarian remake of that old favorite from the south of France.

Serves 4

15 minutes

18–24 minutes

1

SALAD

4	large eggs
8	ounces (250 g) baby potatoes
8	ounces (250 g) green beans, trimmed
3	tomatoes, quartered
3	marinated artichokes, quartered
1	red onion, sliced
¼	cup (25 g) small black olives
¼	cup fresh flat-leaf parsley

DRESSING

2	tablespoons freshly squeezed lemon juice
2	tablespoons extra-virgin olive oil
1	clove garlic, finely chopped
½	teaspoon Dijon mustard
	Salt and freshly ground black pepper

1. **To prepare the salad,** put the eggs in a small saucepan, cover with cold water, and bring to a boil. Decrease the heat to medium and gently simmer for 6 minutes. Drain and cool under cold running water. Peel and quarter.

2. **Steam** the potatoes for 10–15 minutes, until tender. Cut in half and set aside. Meanwhile, bring a medium saucepan of water to a boil, add the beans, and blanch until just tender, 2–3 minutes.

3. **Combine** the eggs, potatoes, and green beans in a medium bowl and add the tomatoes, artichokes, onion, olives, and parsley.

4. **To prepare the dressing,** whisk together the lemon juice, oil, garlic, and mustard in a small bowl. Season with salt and pepper.

5. **Drizzle** the dressing over the salad, toss to combine, and serve.

If you liked this recipe, you will love these as well.

pesto potato salad

40

lentil & herb salad

34

baked veggie salad

38

fruit & nut quinoa salad

Quinoa is a seed crop originally from South America. It is gluten-free and a good source of protein as well as dietary fiber.

Serves 4–6

15 minutes

15 minutes

1

2	cups (500 ml) water
2	cups (400 g) quinoa, rinsed
1½	cups (270 g) dried apricots, sliced
⅓	cup (50 g) almonds, coarsely chopped
⅓	cup (50 g) pistachios
¼	cup (45 g) raisins
¼	cup (45 g) currants
2	tablespoons finely chopped fresh mint
2	tablespoons finely chopped fresh cilantro (coriander)
	Finely grated zest and juice of 1 lemon
2	tablespoons extra-virgin olive oil
1	teaspoon finely grated orange zest
½	teaspoon ground cinnamon
	Salt and freshly ground black pepper

1. **Combine** the water and quinoa in a medium saucepan and bring to a boil. Decrease the heat to low, cover, and simmer until all the water is absorbed, 15 minutes. Fluff the grains with a fork and transfer to a medium bowl.

2. **Add** the apricots, almonds, pistachios, raisins, currants, mint, cilantro, lemon zest and juice, oil, orange zest, and cinnamon.

3. **Stir** to combine. Season with salt and pepper and serve.

If you liked this recipe, you will love these as well.

bulgur with walnuts

98

wheat berries with zucchini & parmesan

102

baked rice salad

Baking the rice in the vegetable broth adds an extra layer of flavor to the finished salad, but if you are short of time you could also use plain boiled rice.

 Serves 4

30 minutes

45–60 minutes

2

1	small onion	1	large red bell pepper (capsicum)
3	cloves	6	pickled gherkins, drained
6	tablespoons extra-virgin olive oil	1	tablespoon salt-cured capers, rinsed
1½	cups (300 g) short-grain rice	3	tablespoons white wine vinegar
1	bay leaf		Salt
	Generous 2⅓ cups (600 ml) vegetable broth, boiling	1	cup (150 g) canned corn (sweet corn), drained
1	cup (150 g) frozen chopped green beans	2	cups (100 g) arugula (rocket)
1	cup (150 g) frozen peas		

1. **Preheat** the oven to 350°F (180°C/gas 4).

2. **Stud** the onion with the cloves. Heat 2 tablespoons of oil in a Dutch oven over medium heat. Add the onion and sauté until transparent, 3–4 minutes.

3. **Stir** in the rice, bay leaf, and broth. Cover and bake for about 20 minutes, until the rice has absorbed the broth and is al dente. Let cool.

4. **Cook** the green beans in salted boiling water until tender, 5–7 minutes. Drain.

5. **Cook** the peas in salted boiling water until tender, 3–5 minutes. Drain.

6. **Preheat** the broiler (grill) to high. Grill the bell pepper until charred all over, 10 minutes. Put in a plastic bag, seal, and let rest for 10 minutes. Peel off the skin and remove the seeds. Wipe clean with paper towels and slice thinly.

7. **Blend** the gherkins, capers, remaining oil, and vinegar in a food processor until smooth.

8. **Put** the rice in a salad bowl. Discard the onion, cloves, and bay leaf. Add the green beans, peas, corn, pepper, and arugula.

9. **Toss** gently with the dressing.

If you liked this recipe, you will love these as well.

rice with tomato pesto & mozzarella

108

rice with herbs & feta

110

vegetarian paella

124

pasta salad
with feta & olives

This pasta salad combines the flavors of a traditional Greek salad with the delicious mellowness of freshly cooked pasta.

- Serves 6
- 15 minutes
- 30 minutes
- 10–12 minutes
- 1

1½ pounds (750 g) cherry tomatoes, quartered
1 small red onion, thinly sliced
1 clove garlic, finely chopped
8 ounces (250 g) feta cheese, cut into small cubes
⅓ cup (90 ml) extra-virgin olive oil
1 tablespoon finely chopped fresh basil + extra leaves to garnish

1 tablespoon finely chopped fresh mint
Finely grated zest of 1 unwaxed lemon
Salt and freshly ground black pepper
1 pound (500 g) penne or other short pasta
1 cup (100 g) black olives, pitted

1. **Combine** the tomatoes, onion, garlic, feta, oil, basil, mint, and lemon zest in a large salad bowl. Toss well and season with salt and pepper. Let rest for 30 minutes.

2. **Cook** the pasta in a large pot of salted boiling water until al dente, 10-12 minutes.

3. **Drain** well and set aside to dry in the colander for 4–5 minutes. Shake the pasta in the colander often so that it doesn't stick together.

4. **Add** the pasta to the bowl with the dressing. Add the olives and toss well.

5. **Garnish** with basil and serve.

If you liked this recipe, you will love these as well.

rigatoni with roasted bell pepper sauce

134

rigatoni with cauliflower

138

farfalle with yogurt & avocado

144

soups

chilled zucchini & yogurt soup

This unusual soup is ideal for hot summer meals and is very healthy. The latest research shows that eating yogurt regularly helps lower blood pressure.

- Serves 4
- 10 minutes
- 1–2 hours
- 45–50 minutes
- 1

12	ounces (350 g) zucchini (courgettes), trimmed
	Salt and freshly ground black pepper
4	tablespoons (60 ml) extra-virgin olive oil
1	head garlic
2/3	cup (150 ml) light (single) cream
2/3	cup (150 ml) low-fat sour cream
1 1/3	cups (300 ml) plain low-fat yogurt
1	tablespoon + 1 teaspoon freshly squeezed lemon juice
1	tablespoon balsamic vinegar
1	tablespoon whole-grain mustard
3	tablespoons fresh mint leaves
1/2	cup (60 g) crushed walnuts + extra, to garnish

1. **Preheat** the oven to 400°F (200°C/gas 6).

2. **Brush** the garlic with 1 tablespoon of oil, wrap in aluminum foil, and roast in a roasting pan in the oven for 45–50 minutes, until very soft.

3. **Season** the zucchini with salt and pepper and brush with 2 tablespoons of the remaining oil. Add to the roasting pan with the garlic after it has been in the oven for about 10 minutes. Set the garlic and zucchini aside for a few minutes, until cool enough to handle.

4. **Cut** the zucchini into chunks and place in a bowl. Squeeze out the soft flesh of the garlic into the bowl, mixing well.

5. **Combine** the zucchini mixture, cream, sour cream, yogurt, 1 tablespoon of lemon juice, vinegar, mustard, and 2 tablespoons of mint in a food processor and chop until smooth. Transfer to a bowl and season with salt and pepper. Chill in the coldest part of the refrigerator for at least 1–2 hours.

6. **Just** before serving, the remaining 1 tablespoon of oil in a small frying pan over medium heat. Add the walnuts, remaining 1 teaspoon of lemon juice, and a pinch of salt and sauté for 2 minutes.

7. **Ladle** the chilled soup into serving bowls, garnish with the remaining mint and the walnut mixture, and serve.

cool cantaloupe soup

Choose cantaloupes with unblemished skins that will look better when serving.

Serves 4

20 minutes

1 hour

1

2	small cantaloupe (rock) melons, weighing about 2 pounds (1 kg) each
	Seeds of 6 cardamom pods
2	leaves fresh basil, torn
1	small fresh green chili, seeded and finely chopped
½	clove garlic

1	bunch fresh dill or chervil, finely chopped
1	tablespoon extra-virgin olive oil
½	teaspoon salt
1	tablespoon freshly squeezed lemon juice

1. **Cut** the melons in half. Scoop out the seeds and fibers and discard. Scoop out the flesh, leaving a ½-inch (1-cm) border. Place the flesh in a bowl. Reserve the shells.

2. **Chop** the cardamom, basil, chili, garlic, and dill in a food processor until they form a smooth pesto (sauce).

3. **Combine** the melon flesh, pesto, oil, and salt in a food processor or blender and process until smooth.

4. **Add** the lemon juice and stir until well blended.

5. **Spoon** the soup into the melon shells and chill in the refrigerator for 1 hour before serving.

If you liked this recipe, you will love these as well.

chilled zucchini & yogurt soup

52

leek & yogurt soup

56

spicy pumpkin & chili soup

60

leek & yogurt soup

This recipe comes from Turkey where yogurt is used in a wide variety of dishes.

Serves 4

20 minutes

25–30 minutes

1

FLAVORED BUTTER

2   tablespoons unsalted butter, softened

½   small clove garlic, crushed

½   teaspoon sweet paprika

¼   teaspoon crushed red pepper flakes

2   teaspoons finely chopped fresh mint

½   teaspoon finely grated lemon zest

SOUP

2   tablespoons butter

3   tablespoons extra-virgin olive oil

4   leeks, trimmed, cut in half lengthwise, and thinly sliced

2   green chiles, seeded and finely sliced, or 1 teaspoon crushed red pepper flakes

1   tablespoon finely chopped fresh mint, or 1 teaspoon dried mint

1   large egg yolk

1½   teaspoons cornstarch (cornflour)

1⅓   cups (350 g) plain Greek-style yogurt

1   teaspoon finely grated lemon zest

2   tablespoons freshly squeezed lemon juice

2   cups (500 ml) water, + more if needed

½   teaspoon salt, + more if needed

½   cup (60–75 g) cooked white rice (optional, for a thicker soup)

     Freshly ground black pepper

1. **To prepare the flavored butter,** beat the butter in a small bowl until light and fluffy. Mix in the garlic, paprika, red pepper flakes, mint, and lemon zest. Press into a log, wrap in plastic wrap (cling film), and chill until needed.

2. **To prepare the soup,** heat the butter and oil in a large soup pot over medium heat. When the butter starts to bubble, stir in the leeks and sauté over low heat for 10 minutes.

3. **Add** the chiles and mint and simmer, stirring frequently, until the leeks are soft and sweet, 10–15 minutes. Remove from the heat.

4. **Whisk** the egg yolk into the cornstarch in a large bowl. Stir in the yogurt and add the lemon zest, half the lemon juice, water, and salt. Whisk until all the ingredients are combined (it should be the consistency of light cream). Thin with a little more water, if needed.

5. **Add** this mixture to the leeks in the soup pot. Stir in the cooked rice, if using. Gently heat the soup over medium-low heat, stirring every now and then. Don't let the mixture boil.

6. **Check** the seasoning and add salt, pepper, and more lemon juice to taste.

7. **To finish,** melt the flavored butter in a small pan over low heat.

8. **Drizzle** the flavored butter over the soup just before serving.

quick three-bean soup
with basil butter & croutons

This delicious soup is quick and easy to prepare. Beans are packed with dietary fiber, making this soup a healthy dish that is perfect for weeknight suppers.

Serves 6

10 minutes

15–20 minutes

1

BASIL-BUTTER GARNISH

¼	cup (60 g) melted butter
3	tablespoons finely chopped fresh basil
½	teaspoon finely grated lemon zest
1	teaspoon fresh lemon juice

SOUP

2	tablespoons extra-virgin olive oil
1	onion, chopped
2	cloves garlic, sliced
	Salt and freshly ground black pepper
1	large potato, diced
1	(14-ounce/400-g) can butter or lima beans, drained
1	(14-ounce/400-g) can cannellini beans, drained
1	(14-ounce/400-g) can kidney beans, drained
5	cups (1.25 liters) vegetable stock
1	teaspoon sweet paprika
1	bay leaf
1	tablespoon finely chopped fresh basil
2	tablespoons freshly squeezed lemon juice

1. **To prepare the basil-butter garnish,** mix all the ingredients in a small bowl and chill until needed.

2. **To prepare the soup,** heat the oil in a large soup pot over medium heat, add the onion and garlic, and sauté until softened, about 5 minutes. Season with salt and pepper.

3. **Add** the potato, beans, stock, paprika, and bay leaf. Stir and bring to a boil. Simmer gently, uncovered, until the potato is tender, 10–15 minutes.

4. **Remove** the bay leaf and stir in the parsley and basil. Remove from the heat and chop until smooth with a handheld mixer or in a blender.

5. **Return** to the pot, if necessary, and add the lemon juice and some boiling water if it is too thick. Season with salt and pepper to taste.

6. **Reheat** the soup gently then ladle into individual dishes.

7. **Float** a disk of basil butter on top of each serving, and serve with croutons.

If you liked this recipe, you will love these as well.

lentil soup with cumin & swiss chard

68

fava bean, pasta & bell pepper soup

86

mixed bean & farro soup in bread rolls

92

spicy pumpkin & chili soup

If you are not fond of spicy food, remember that this soup is equally good without the chili and red pepper flakes. Just omit them and prepare as usual.

Serves 6

20 minutes

40 minutes

1

¼	cup (60 g) butter
1	large onion, chopped
2	cloves garlic, sliced
2	pounds (1 kg) pumpkin or butternut squash, peeled, seeded, and cubed
1	potato or sweet potato, diced
1	fresh red chili, seeded and sliced
2	teaspoons coriander seeds
1	tablespoon cumin seeds

1	teaspoon red pepper flakes
1	teaspoon smoked paprika (pimentòn)
5	cups (1.25 liters) vegetable stock
	Freshly squeezed juice of 1 lime
	Salt and freshly ground black pepper
2	tablespoons chopped fresh cilantro (coriander)
6	tablespoons (90 ml) plain yogurt, to serve

1. **Melt** the butter in a soup pot over medium-low heat. Add the onion and garlic and sauté until softened, 3–4 minutes.

2. **Add** the pumpkin, potato, and chili. Cook until the pumpkin is golden at the edges, 5–6 minutes.

3. **Toast** the coriander and cumin seeds in a pan over low heat until fragrant, 1–2 minutes. Grind with a pestle and mortar.

4. **Stir** the toasted spices, red pepper flakes, and paprika into the pumpkin mixture and simmer for 1–2 minutes.

5. **Add** the vegetable stock, cover, and simmer until the pumpkin is tender, about 20 minutes.

6. **Purée** the soup in a food processor. Return to the pan and stir in the lime juice. Season with salt and pepper, and additional pepper flakes for extra spice, if desired. Reheat the soup gently and stir in most of the cilantro.

7. **Sprinkle** with the remaining cilantro, add a swirl of yogurt, and serve.

If you liked this recipe, you will love these as well.

quick butternut squash soup

62

pumpkin fritters

194

pumpkin & lentil tagine

222

sweet butternut squash soup

The caramelized seeds add an extra sweet touch to this soup. Use butternut squash if buttercup or kuri is not available.

Serves 6

30 minutes

75 minutes

2

CARAMELIZED SQUASH SEEDS

1/2	cup (60 g) butternut squash seeds (from squash below)
1	tablespoon maple syrup
1	teaspoon brown sugar
1/4	teaspoon salt
1	tablespoon sunflower oil
	Pinch cayenne pepper

SOUP

1	butternut squash or pumpkin (about 1 1/2 pounds/ 750 g)
1	small buttercup or red kuri squash
3	tablespoons unsalted butter
	Salt and freshly ground black pepper
4	sprigs of marjoram
3/4	cup (200 ml) boiling water
	Pinch of saffron
1	large leek, thinly sliced
1	teaspoon salt
2	medium sweet potatoes, peeled and cut into 3/4-inch (2-cm) cubes
1/2	teaspoon ground cinnamon
1/4	teaspoon ground cloves
1/2	teaspoon ground cumin or cumin seeds, roasted and lightly ground
2 1/2	inches (8 cm) fresh ginger, peeled and finely grated
4	cups (1 liter) vegetable broth, warmed
3/4	cup (200 ml) milk
1/4	teaspoon freshly grated nutmeg
2	tablespoons finely chopped fresh cilantro (coriander)

1. **To prepare the squash seeds,** preheat the oven to 375°F (190°C/gas 5). Cut the squash in half and scoop out the seeds, discarding the fibers. Rinse the seeds and dry on a cloth.

2. **Mix** all the seed ingredients in a small bowl. Line a baking sheet with parchment paper and brush with sunflower oil. Spread the seeds out on the baking sheet and bake for 10–15 minutes, until golden. Let cool.

3. **To prepare the soup,** dot the insides of the squash halves with 1 tablespoon of butter. Season with salt and pepper, and place a sprig of marjoram in each. Place in a roasting pan, skin side up, and add 1/2 cup (120 ml) of water. Roast for 35–40 minutes, until tender.

4. **Mix** the saffron in a small bow with 2 tablespoons of water. Set aside.

5. **Heat** the remaining butter in a large soup pot over medium-low heat until beginning to bubble. Add the leek, salt, and remaining 2 tablespoons of water. Cover and simmer for 10 minutes, stirring frequently.

6. **Mix** in the sweet potatoes, cinnamon, cloves, cumin, ginger, and saffron mixture. Stir well. Pour in the stock, cover, and simmer for 10 minutes.

7. **Scoop** the flesh out of the squash and add to the soup, along with the juices from the pan. Bring back to a boil and simmer for 10 minutes. Take off the heat and purée with a handheld blender or in a food processor.

8. **Return** to the pan and add the milk and nutmeg. Gently reheat. Serve hot, with the cilantro, black pepper, and caramelized seeds.

pea soup
with mint pesto toasts

Traditional pesto is an Italian basil sauce usually served with pasta. In our pesto recipe we have replaced the basil with mint and parsley and spread them on toast to serve as croutons with the pea soup.

Serves 6

20 minutes

25 minutes

1

SOUP

2 tablespoons extra-virgin olive oil
2 onions, chopped
2 small cloves garlic, coarsely chopped
1 leek, finely chopped
1 potato, peeled and diced
1/2 teaspoon curry powder
1/2 teaspoon finely grated lemon zest
1 pound (500 g) frozen peas, thawed
2 cups (500 ml) vegetable stock

3 tablespoons chopped fresh mint
1/4 cup (60 ml) cream
Salt

MINT PESTO TOASTS

2 tablespoons pine nuts
1/2 cup (25 g) fresh mint
1/2 cup (25 g) fresh parsley
1 clove garlic, peeled
1/4 cup (60 ml) extra-virgin olive oil
2 tablespoons freshly grated pecorino
1 baguette (French loaf), sliced and toasted

1. **To prepare the soup,** heat the oil in a soup pot over medium heat. Add the onions and sauté until softened, 3–4 minutes. Stir in the garlic, leek, potato, curry powder, and lemon zest and simmer over low heat for 5 minutes.

2. **Add** the peas and stock. Bring to a boil, cover, and simmer until the potato is soft, 10–15 minutes. Remove from the heat and stir in the mint.

3. **To prepare the mint pesto toasts,** chop the pine nuts, mint, parsley, garlic, and oil in a food processor until

puréed. Transfer to a small bowl and stir in the pecorino. Add a pinch of salt. Cover with plastic wrap (cling film) and refrigerate.

4. **Remove** the soup from the heat and purée with a handheld blender or in a food processor until smooth.

5. **Return** to the heat and stir in the cream. Gently reheat.

6. **Spread** the pesto on the toasts and float on the soup. Serve hot.

If you liked this recipe, you will love these as well.

green bean & almond soup

72

broccoli soup with cheese toasts

80

vegetable soup with pasta & pesto

84

portuguese caldo verde
with croutons

Caldo verde is a traditional Portuguese vegetable soup. There are many variations on the classic recipe; this is our favorite.

Serves 6

15 minutes

35–40 minutes

1

SOUP

1	tablespoon extra-virgin olive oil
1	medium onion, coarsely chopped
2	cloves garlic, finely chopped
2	carrots, cut into ½-inch (1-cm) cubes
2	stalks celery, cut into small pieces
1	teaspoon salt
½	teaspoon smoked paprika (pimentòn)
1½	pounds (750 g) potatoes, peeled and cut into small cubes
5	cups (1.25 liters) water
1	pound (500 g) kale or white cabbage, thinly sliced
	Salt and freshly ground black pepper

CROUTONS

2	slices bread, cut into ½-inch (1-cm) cubes
¼	cup (60 g) butter
2	tablespoons finely chopped fresh parsley

1. **To prepare the soup,** heat the oil in a large soup pot over medium heat. Add the onion, garlic, carrots, celery, salt, and paprika. Decrease the heat, cover the pan, and sweat the vegetables until almost tender, 8–10 minutes, stirring once or twice.

2. **Add** the potatoes and water. Bring to a boil, cover, and simmer over low heat until tender, about 15 minutes.

3. **Place** the cabbage in a colander and pour boiling water over to wilt. Set aside.

4. **Purée** the soup with a handheld blender or in a blender until almost smooth.

5. **Return** to the heat, add the cabbage, and bring back to a boil. Simmer until the cabbage is tender, 6–8 minutes.

6. **Season** with salt and pepper.

7. **To prepare the croutons,** fry the bread in the butter over medium heat until golden, 3–4 minutes. Season with salt and pepper.

8. **Ladle** the soup into bowls and top with the croutons. Garnish with the parsley, and serve hot.

lentil soup
with cumin & swiss chard

You can make this Lebanese soup with spinach instead of chard. There is no need to blanch spinach because the leaves are more tender than the chard.

Serves 4

15 minutes

50–55 minutes

1

2	cups (200 g) small brown or dark green lentils	2	pounds (1 kg) Swiss chard (silverbeet)
5	cups (1.25 liters) water, + more if needed	3	cloves garlic, sliced
	Parmesan rind (optional)		Freshly ground black pepper
1	bay leaf		Freshly squeezed juice of 1 lemon
6	tablespoons (90 ml) extra-virgin olive oil		Pita bread, toasted and cut into squares, to serve
1	medium onion, thinly sliced		
	Salt		
1	teaspoon cumin seeds, coarsely ground		

1. **Wash** the lentils and transfer to a large soup pot with the water. Bring to a boil, add the Parmesan rind, if using, and bay leaf, and simmer until tender, 30–40 minutes.

2. **While** the lentils are cooking, heat 3 tablespoons of the oil in a frying pan over medium heat. Add the onion and a pinch of salt and sauté until golden, 6–8 minutes. Stir in the cumin and set aside.

3. **Separate** the chard leaves from the stems and cut the stems into ½-inch (1-cm) pieces.

4. **Bring** a large pan of salted water to a boil and add the chard stems and leaves. Bring back to a boil quickly and simmer until tender, 2–3 minutes. Refresh in cold running water. Drain and squeeze gently to remove excess water. Chop coarsely.

5. **Heat** the remaining 3 tablespoons of oil in a large pan over medium heat. Add the garlic and sauté until golden, 3–4 minutes.

6. **Add** the chard and toss briefly in the oil. Season with salt and pepper and remove from the heat. Remove the bay leaf and Parmesan rind from the cooked lentils. Add the fried onion to the pot and stir.

7. **Purée** the lentil mixture with a handheld blender or in a food processor until almost smooth.

8. **Return** to the soup pot, stir in the braised chard, and reheat over low heat. If the soup is too thick, add more hot water.

9. **Stir** in the lemon juice and season with salt and pepper.

10. **Serve** hot with the pita bread.

kasha soup
with wild mushrooms

Kasha, also known as buckwheat, is a popular cereal in Russia and other eastern European countries and also in the United States.

Serves 4

20 minutes

35 minutes

1

¼	cup (60 ml) extra-virgin olive oil	
1	medium onion, finely chopped	
6	ounces (180 g) mixed wild mushrooms, thinly sliced	
2	cloves garlic, finely chopped	
1	cup (150 g) kasha (buckwheat groats)	

1	bay leaf
4	cups (1 liter) water
	Salt and freshly ground black pepper
¼	cup (60 ml) sour cream, to garnish
1	tablespoon finely chopped fresh thyme, to garnish

1. **Heat** the oil in a large saucepan over medium heat. Add the onion and sauté until softened, about 5 minutes.

2. **Stir** in the mushrooms and garlic. Sauté until the mushrooms have softened slightly, about 5 minutes.

3. **Add** the kasha and bay leaf. Pour in the water.

4. **Bring** to a boil, lower the heat, and simmer until the kasha is tender and the mushrooms are cooked, about 20 minutes.

5. **Season** with salt and pepper. Swirl in the sour cream and garnish with the thyme. Remove the bay leaf.

6. **Serve** hot.

If you liked this recipe, you will love these as well.

mixed bean & farro soup in bread rolls

92

bulgur with walnuts

98

wheat berries with zucchini & parmesan

102

green bean & almond soup

Low in calories and packed with dietary fiber and essential vitamins and minerals, green beans are always a healthy food choice.

Serves 4

10 minutes

15–20 minutes

1

¼	cup (60 g) butter
1	medium onion, finely chopped
1	large clove garlic, finely chopped
1	tablespoon all-purpose (plain) flour
3	cups (750 ml) vegetable stock or water
12	ounces (350 g) fresh thin green beans, trimmed
1	tablespoon coarsely chopped fresh parsley + extra, to garnish
1	teaspoon coarsely chopped fresh chervil
2	fresh sage leaves, coarsely chopped (optional)
2	teaspoons freshly squeezed lemon juice
	Salt and freshly ground black pepper
⅔	cup (60 g) blanched almonds, coarsely chopped

1. **Melt** half the butter in a medium soup pot over low heat. Add the onion and garlic and sauté until soft but not browned, about 5 minutes.

2. **Stir** in the flour and mix well. Add about half the stock, little by little, stirring all the time. Bring to a simmer and add the beans and herbs.

3. **Cook** until the beans are just tender, 5–8 minutes. Set aside to cool then purée the soup with a handheld blender in a food processor.

4. **Return** to the pot and use the remaining stock, plus extra water, to dilute the soup to a creamy consistency.

5. **Reheat** and taste for seasoning, adding lemon juice, salt, and pepper. Don't let the soup boil.

6. **Fry** the almonds in the remaining butter in a small frying pan, stirring until golden brown. Mix into the soup and serve hot garnished with parsley.

If you liked this recipe, you will love these as well.

pea soup with mint pesto toasts

64

broccoli soup with cheese toasts

80

vegetable soup with pasta & pesto

84

creamy czech mushroom soup

This Czech soup, called *kulajda* in its homeland, is traditionally served with hard-boiled eggs.

Serves 4

20–25 minutes

20–25 minutes

1

3	tablespoons corn oil
8	ounces (250 g) fresh chestnut or white button mushrooms, thinly sliced
½	teaspoon caraway seeds
3	tablespoons finely chopped fresh dill
	Salt and freshly ground black pepper
2	tablespoons unsalted butter
⅓	cup (50 g) all-purpose (plain) flour

2½	cups (700 ml) hot water
1	teaspoon sugar
1	tablespoon white wine vinegar
¾	cup (200 ml) sour cream
4	hard-boiled eggs, shelled and halved (optional)
1	tablespoon snipped fresh chives, to garnish

1. **Heat** 2 tablespoons of the oil in a soup pot over medium heat. Add the mushrooms and caraway seeds and sauté until the mushrooms soften, 5–7 minutes.

2. **Remove** from the heat, stir in half the dill, and season with salt and pepper. Transfer to a bowl.

3. **In** the same pot, melt the butter with the remaining oil over medium heat and add the flour, stirring until the mixture turns into a pale paste.

4. **Gradually** pour in the hot water and ½ teaspoon salt and stir until smooth. Simmer for 10–15 minutes.

5. **Mix** in the mushrooms and bring back to a boil. Stir in the sugar, vinegar, and remaining dill. Add salt and pepper and simmer for 1–2 minutes.

6. **Stir** in the sour cream. Gently reheat without boiling.

7. **Put** the eggs in individual dishes and ladle the soup over the top. Garnish with the chives, and serve hot.

If you liked this recipe, you will love these as well.

kasha soup with wild mushrooms

70

polenta with mushrooms

132

fusilli with mushrooms

140

spiced tomato soup

This tasty soup looks very attractive with its decorative tomato skin topping.

Serves 6

15–20 minutes

25–35 minutes

1

2	pounds (1 kg) ripe tomatoes	½	teaspoon sugar
2	tablespoons extra-virgin olive oil	⅓	cup (90 ml) dry white wine
1	red onion, coarsely chopped	1⅔	cups (400 ml) water
1	small leek, sliced	1	tablespoon puréed sun-dried tomato
2	cloves garlic, chopped	¼	teaspoon ground cumin
1	small fresh red chili, seeded and finely chopped		Dash of Tabasco
1	carrot, sliced	1	tablespoon fresh thyme, chopped
1	potato, diced	1	tablespoon freshly squeezed lemon juice
	Salt and freshly ground black pepper	3	tablespoons sunflower oil

1. **Plunge** the tomatoes into boiling water, leave for 1 minute, drain, then peel. Reserve the skins. Coarsely chop the tomatoes.

2. **Heat** the olive oil in a large soup pot over low heat. Add the onion and leek and sauté until softened, 3–4 minutes.

3. **Add** the garlic, chili, carrot, potato, and 1 teaspoon salt. Cover and simmer over low heat for 10 minutes.

4. **Stir** in the tomatoes, sugar, and wine. Increase the heat and stir for 2 minutes.

5. **Add** enough water to just cover the vegetables and bring to a boil. Simmer

uncovered for 10–15 minutes, until the vegetables are soft.

6. **Purée** in a food processor or using a handheld blender and return to the pot. Stir in the sun-dried tomato purée, cumin, Tabasco, thyme, and lemon juice.

7. **Heat** the sunflower oil in a small pan over medium heat. Add the tomato skins and fry for 10–15 seconds. Drain on paper towels.

8. **Serve** the soup hot, topped with tomato skins.

If you liked this recipe, you will love these as well.

spicy pumpkin & chili soup

60

tuscan bread soup

78

corn chowder with potatoes & bell peppers

82

tuscan bread soup

This soup is known as *pappa al pomodoro* in Tuscany where it comes from.

Serves 6

20 minutes

40 minutes

2

3 large red bell peppers (capsicums)
¼ cup (60 ml) extra-virgin olive oil
2 cloves garlic, finely chopped
1½ pounds (750 g) ripe tomatoes, chopped
8 ounces (250 g) firm-textured white bread, crusts removed and crumbled

3 cups (750 ml) vegetable stock
Freshly ground black pepper and salt
2 tablespoons finely chopped fresh basil, + extra leaves to garnish
2 tablespoons finely chopped fresh marjoram or oregano

1. **Preheat** the broiler (grill) on a high setting. Grill the bell peppers, turning them from time to time, until they are charred all over. Remove from the grill and transfer to a plastic bag. Seal the bag and let rest for 10 minutes. Remove the peppers from the bag. Peel and discard the seeds. Thinly slice the bell peppers.

2. **Heat** the oil in a large saucepan over medium heat. Add the garlic and sauté until pale golden brown, 3–4 minutes.

3. **Add** the tomatoes and half the bell peppers. Bring to a boil.

4. **Add** the bread and mix well. Add the vegetable stock and mix well. Season with black pepper and bring to a boil. Simmer until the bread has broken down, about 15 minutes. Season with salt and add the basil and marjoram.

5. **Ladle** into serving bowls and top with the remaining peppers. Garnish with basil. Serve hot.

If you liked this recipe, you will love these as well.

spicy pumpkin & chili soup

60

spiced tomato soup

76

minestrone

94

broccoli soup
with cheese toasts

Broccoli is a very good source of vitamins K and C, and many other nutrients as well. Regular consumption is believed to help prevent and treat chronic inflammation in the body and to cut the risk of cancer.

Serves 4

20 minutes

25 minutes

1

1	large head broccoli (about 2 pounds/1 kg)		Salt and freshly ground white pepper
4	tablespoons (60 ml) extra-virgin olive oil	4	slices bread, cut in fingers or small squares
2	cloves garlic, finely chopped	½	cup (60 g) freshly grated cheddar or Emmental cheese
1	large potato, peeled and diced		
6	cups (1.5 liters) vegetable broth	2	tablespoons diced red bell pepper (capsicum)

1. **Separate** the broccoli into florets. Finely chop the stalk and coarsely chop the leaves.

2. **Heat** 2 tablespoons of the oil in a large soup pot over high heat. Add the garlic and sauté until soft, 2–3 minutes.

3. **Add** the broccoli, (leaves, florets, and stalks), potato, and broth. Season with salt and white pepper. Partially cover and simmer over low heat until the broccoli is tender, about 15 minutes.

4. **Remove** from the heat, let cool slightly, and purée with a handheld

blender or in a food processor until smooth.

5. **Reheat** the soup, then ladle into soup bowls.

6. **Preheat** the broiler (grill). Sprinkle the sliced bread with the cheese and bell pepper and broil until the cheese has melted, 3–5 minutes.

7. **Float** the toasts on the soup, and serve hot.

If you liked this recipe, you will love these as well.

pea soup with mint pesto toasts
64

green bean & almond soup
72

vegetable soup with pasta & pesto
84

corn chowder
with potatoes & bell peppers

In this recipe, we have enriched a traditional corn chowder with more vegetables.

Serves 6–8

25 minutes

25–35 minutes

2

3	tablespoons extra-virgin olive oil
2	onions, chopped
2	cloves garlic, finely chopped
1	mild fresh green chile, seeded and finely chopped
1	stalk celery, sliced
1	carrot, thinly sliced
1	teaspoon salt
1	tablespoon cornstarch (cornflour), dissolved in ¼ cup (60 ml) water
1	pound (500 g) new potatoes, thinly sliced

1	pound (500 g) frozen corn (sweet corn)
1	teaspoon tomato paste (concentrate)
8	cups (2 liters) vegetable stock
2	red bell peppers (capsicums), seeded and diced
2	tablespoons finely chopped fresh basil
1	tablespoon finely chopped fresh parsley

1. **Heat** the oil in a large soup pot over medium heat. Add the onions, garlic, chile, celery, and carrot and sauté until softened, about 5 minutes.

2. **Add** the salt. Cover and cook until the vegetables are tender, 5–10 minutes. Add the cornstarch mixture and stir until blended.

3. **Add** the potatoes and corn. Dissolve the tomato paste in 4 cups (1 liter) of the vegetable stock. Whisk the mixture into the vegetables.

4. **Bring** to a boil and simmer until the potatoes are just tender but not mushy, 8–10 minutes.

5. **Add** the bell peppers and pour in the remaining 4 cups (1 liter) of stock. Return to a gentle boil. Stir in the basil and parsley, and serve hot.

If you liked this recipe, you will love these as well.

vegetable soup with pasta & pesto

84

fava bean, pasta & bell pepper soup

86

roasted summer vegetable soup

90

vegetable soup
with pasta & pesto

This soup mimics the flavors of a traditional pasta dish from Genoa, in northwestern Italy. See our version of the recipe on page 152.

Serves 6

10 minutes

30 minutes

1

PESTO

1	cup (50 g) fresh basil leaves
¼	cup (45 g) pine nuts
2	cloves garlic, peeled
½	cup (60 g) freshly grated Parmesan cheese
⅓	cup (90 ml) extra-virgin olive oil

SOUP

8	cups (2 liters) vegetable stock
12	ounces (350 g) green beans, topped, tailed, and cut in short lengths
2	large waxy (boiling) potatoes, peeled and cut into small cubes
	Salt and freshly ground black pepper
8	ounces (250 g) small bow ties or other small soup pasta

1. **To prepare the pesto,** chop the basil, pine nuts, and garlic in a food processor and purée until smooth. Add the cheese and oil and mix well.

2. **To prepare the soup,** bring the vegetable stock to a boil in a large soup pot over medium heat. Add the green beans and potatoes. Season with salt and pepper and simmer for 15 minutes.

3. **Add** the pasta and cook until al dente and the vegetables are very tender, 5–7 minutes.

4. **Add** the pesto and mix well. Ladle into serving bowls, and serve hot.

If you liked this recipe, you will love these as well.

tuscan bread soup

78

minestrone

94

whole-wheat spaghetti with pesto, potatoes & beans

152

fava bean, pasta & bell pepper soup

The bell peppers add a delicious flavor to this soup. If you are pushed for time, use well-drained bell peppers from a jar instead of grilling them yourself.

- Serves 6
- 30 minutes
- 30 minutes

- 2

1	pound (500 g) shelled fresh fava (broad) beans (about 3 pounds/1.5 kg in pods)
1	large or 2 small red bell peppers (capsicums), halved lengthwise and seeded
2	tablespoons light extra-virgin olive oil
2	medium onions, finely chopped
1	cup (150 g) frozen peas
4	cups (1 liter) vegetable broth, warmed
2	cups (100 g) cooked pasta, chopped if large or long
	Salt and freshly ground black pepper
	Freshly grated Parmesan cheese

1. **If** the fava beans are big, remove the tough skins: Put the beans in a pan of boiling water, bring to a simmer, and drain at once. Refresh under cold water, let dry a little, then press gently to slip off the skin.

2. **Place** the bell pepper halves skin side up under a very hot broiler (grill) until blackened. Put in a plastic bag and leave for 10 minutes.

3. **Peel** off the charred skin. Cut the peppers into thin strips and set aside.

4. **Heat** the oil in a large pan over medium heat. Add the onion and sauté until just golden, about 5 minutes. Add the beans and peas and sauté for 2 minutes.

5. **Pour in** the stock, bring to a boil, and simmer over low heat until tender, 10–12 minutes. Add the pasta, bring back to a boil, and simmer for 2 minutes.

6. **Stir** in the bell peppers and season with salt and pepper. Serve with Parmesan sprinkled on top.

If you liked this recipe, you will love these as well.

vegetable soup with pasta & pesto

84

viennese potato soup

88

roasted summer vegetable soup

90

viennese potato soup

The porcini mushrooms add a wonderful flavor to this soup.

- Serves 4
- 20 minutes
- 20 minutes
- 30-40 minutes

- 1

½	ounce (15 g) dried porcini or ceps
5	cups (1.25 liters) hot water
1	teaspoon salt, + more if needed
4	large potatoes, peeled and cut into small cubes
2	celery stalks, sliced
1	carrot, diced
2	tablespoons butter
1	onion, finely chopped
1	tablespoon all-purpose (plain) flour
1	teaspoon finely grated lemon zest
1	clove garlic, sliced
¼	teaspoon dried marjoram
½	teaspoon caraway seeds
	Freshly ground black pepper
4	tablespoons (60 ml) sour cream
2	tablespoons finely chopped fresh parsley

1. **Put** the porcini in a small bowl with enough warm water to cover. Soak for 20 minutes.

2. **Combine** the potato, celery, and carrot in a large soup pot and add the remaining water and salt.

3. **Chop** the porcini and add to the pot with their soaking liquid. Bring to a boil and simmer until tender, about 20 minutes.

4. **Melt** the butter in a frying pan over medium heat. Add the onion and sauté until softened, 3–4 minutes.

5. **Stir** in the flour until a light brown paste forms, about 2 minutes.

6. **Mix** in the lemon zest, garlic, marjoram, and caraway seeds. Pour in a ladleful of the vegetable liquid, stirring until thickened.

7. **Scrape** the contents from the frying pan into the soup pot and mix in well. Simmer for 5 minutes. Season with salt and pepper.

9. **Serve** hot with sour cream and parsley.

If you liked this recipe, you will love these as well.

fava bean, pasta & bell pepper soup

86

mixed bean & farro soup in bread rolls

92

roasted summer vegetable soup

90

roasted summer vegetable soup

Vary the vegetables in this soup according to what you like and have on hand.

Serves 6

20 minutes

40 minutes

1

3	zucchini (courgettes), sliced	8	tomatoes, quartered
1	large red onion, sliced	2	tablespoons fresh thyme leaves
3	shallots, peeled	4	cloves garlic, chopped
1	red bell pepper (capsicum), seeded and cut into chunks		Salt and freshly ground black pepper
1	yellow bell pepper (capsicum), seeded and cut into chunks	½	cup (125 ml) extra-virgin olive oil
2	small eggplant (aubergines), chopped	6	cups (1.5 liters) vegetable broth
1	fennel bulb, cut into thick slices		Cabbage leaves cut into thin strips
1	celery root (celeriac), peeled and cut into wedges	1	fresh red chili, thinly sliced

1. **Preheat** the oven to 400°F (200°C/gas 6). Combine the zucchini, onion, shallots, bell peppers, eggplant, fennel, celery root, and tomatoes in a large roasting pan. Sprinkle with thyme, garlic, 1 tablespoon salt, and ½ teaspoon pepper. Drizzle with ⅓ cup (90 ml) of oil and mix well to coat. Roast for 30 minutes, stirring 2 or 3 times, until all the vegetables are soft.

2. **Pour** half the broth into the roasting pan and bring to a boil over medium heat.

3. **Chop** the mixture in a food processor—it should still be grainy.

4. **Transfer** to a large soup pot and stir in the remaining broth. Adjust the seasoning and simmer for 5 minutes.

5. **Heat** the remaining oil in a large frying pan. Stir in the cabbage and cook with the chile and salt until the cabbage softens but retains some bite, 3–4 minutes.

6. **Serve** hot, topped with the cabbage.

If you liked this recipe, you will love these as well.

corn chowder with potatoes & bell peppers

82

fava bean, pasta & bell pepper soup

86

viennese potato soup

88

mixed bean & farro soup
in bread rolls

Farro is an ancient strain of wheat which has been grown in Italy for centuries. Chefs prize it for its nutty flavor, delicate chew, and versatility. It is especially good in soups as it does not become mushy during cooking.

Serves 6

40 minutes

55–65 minutes

1

1	tablespoon extra-virgin olive oil
1	onion, finely chopped
1	carrot, finely chopped
1	stalk celery, finely chopped
¾	cup (100 g) farro
2	cloves garlic, finely chopped
1	teaspoon finely chopped fresh rosemary
1	teaspoon finely chopped fresh sage

4	cherry tomatoes
4	cups (1 liter) vegetable stock
6	large round whole-wheat (wholemeal or 5-cereal) crusty bread rolls
1	(14-ounce/400-g) can mixed beans, or cannellini

1. **Heat** the oil in a large soup pot over medium heat. Add the onion, carrot, and celery and sauté until the onion is lightly browned, about 5 minutes.

2. **Add** the farro, garlic, rosemary, sage, and tomatoes and pour in the vegetable broth. Cover and simmer over low heat until the farro is tender, 30–40 minutes.

3. **Cut** the tops off the bread rolls and remove the bread interior. Cut the interior into small cubes.

4. **Toast** the bread cubes in a nonstick frying pan until lightly browned, about 5 minutes.

5. **Add** the beans and toasted bread cubes to the soup and return to a gentle simmer.

6. **Spoon** the soup into the rolls, place the rolls on serving plates, and serve hot.

If you liked this recipe, you will love these as well.

corn chowder with potatoes & bell peppers

82

viennese potato soup

88

roasted summer vegetable soup

90

minestrone

This classic Italian soup is hearty enough to make a meal in itself.

Serves 6

25 minutes

30–35 minutes

2

2	tablespoons extra-virgin olive oil	¾	cup (130 g) small pasta shapes
1	red onion, diced	2	medium zucchini (courgettes), diced
2	stalks celery, diced	¼	Savoy or green cabbage, coarsely chopped
2	cloves garlic, finely chopped		
1	large carrot, diced	¼	cup finely chopped fresh flat-leaf parsley
2	medium potatoes, peeled and diced		Salt and freshly ground black pepper
1	(14-ounce/400-g) can tomatoes, with juice	⅓	cup (50 g) freshly grated Parmesan
2	tablespoons tomato paste		
1	(14-ounce/400-g) can borlotti or red kidney beans, drained		
5	cups (1.25 liters) vegetable stock		

1. **Heat** the oil in a large, heavy saucepan over medium-high heat. Add the onion, celery, and garlic and cook until golden, about 5 minutes.

2. **Add** the carrot and potato, and cook for 3–4 minutes, until they begin to color. Add the tomatoes, tomato paste, and beans and stir to combine. Pour in the broth and bring to a boil.

3. **Add** the pasta, zucchini, and cabbage, decrease the heat to medium-low, and gently simmer until the pasta and vegetables are cooked, 20–25 minutes. Stir in the parsley. Season with salt and pepper.

4. **Serve** hot with the Parmesan.

If you liked this recipe, you will love these as well.

tuscan bread soup
78

fava bean, pasta & bell pepper soup
86

mixed bean & farro soup in bread rolls
92

grains

bulgur with walnuts

Bulgur is made by soaking and cooking whole-wheat kernels, drying them, removing part of the bran, and then cracking the kernels into smaller pieces. Rich in dietary fiber, vitamins, and minerals, bulgur is more nutritious than white rice or couscous.

Serves 4

20 minutes

30 minutes

1

1⅓	cups (200 g) fine or medium bulgur
1½	cups (150 g) shelled walnuts
½	teaspoon salt
1	onion, finely chopped
20	cherry tomatoes, halved
2	tablespoons finely chopped fresh mint
2	tablespoons extra-virgin olive oil
1	cup (250 ml) plain yogurt
1	clove garlic, finely chopped

1. **Soak** the bulgur in 2½ cups (600 ml) boiling water for 15 minutes.

2. **Line** a colander with a clean kitchen towel. Drain the bulgur, using the towel to squeeze out as much moisture as possible.

3. **Chop** the walnuts coarsely with the salt on a chopping board. Mix the bulgur, walnuts, onion, tomatoes, and mint in a large bowl. Drizzle with the oil.

4. **Refrigerate** for 15 minutes.

5. **Mix** the yogurt and garlic in a small bowl. Chill in the refrigerator until you are ready to serve. Serve the bulgur with the garlic-flavored yogurt.

If you liked this recipe, you will love these as well.

falafel with tabbouleh
100

spiced couscous with mushrooms
104

couscous with roasted vegetables
106

falafel with tabbouleh

Serve these two classic Lebanese dishes as a starter or light lunch. They go beautifully together. You may also like to try them stuffed into pita bread.

Serves 4

45 minutes

15 minutes

20–25 minutes

2

TABBOULEH

½	cup (100 g) fine or medium bulgur
2	medium tomatoes, diced
1	cucumber, halved lengthwise, seeded, and diced
1	small red onion, diced
1	cup (50 g) finely chopped fresh flat-leaf parsley
½	cup (25 g) finely chopped fresh mint

DRESSING

¼	cup (60 ml) freshly squeezed lemon juice
2	tablespoons extra-virgin olive oil
1	tablespoon finely grated lemon zest
1	garlic clove, finely chopped
	Salt and freshly ground black pepper

FALAFEL

1½	teaspoons coriander seeds
1½	teaspoons cumin seeds
1	(14-ounce/400-g) can garbanzo beans (chickpeas), drained
½	small onion, chopped
⅓	cup fresh parsley leaves
2	tablespoons fresh cilantro (coriander)
1	clove garlic, coarsely chopped
1	large green chili, seeded and chopped
	Pinch of cayenne pepper
	Salt and freshly ground black pepper
1	cup (250 ml) vegetable oil, for frying
½	cup (120 ml) plain yogurt, to serve

1. **To prepare the tabbouleh,** soak the bulgur in 1 cup (250 ml) of boiling water for 15 minutes. Line a colander with a clean cloth. Drain the bulgur, using the cloth to squeeze out as much moisture as possible.

2. **Transfer** the bulgur to a bowl and add the tomatoes, cucumber, onion, parsley, and mint.

3. **To prepare the dressing,** whisk the lemon juice, oil, lemon zest, and garlic in a bowl. Pour over the tabbouleh. Season with salt and pepper.

4. **To prepare the falafel,** dry-fry the coriander and cumin seeds in a small frying pan over medium heat until fragrant, about 1 minute. Transfer to a mortar and pestle and pound to a powder.

5. **Chop** the beans, onion, parsley, cilantro, garlic, chili, spices, and cayenne in a food processor until smooth. Season with salt and pepper. Shape into walnut-size balls and press lightly to flatten.

6. **Heat** the oil in a large frying pan over medium-high heat, until hot enough to brown a piece of bread when tested.

7. **Cook** the falafel in batches, until crisp and golden brown, 3–5 minutes on each side. Remove using a slotted spoon and drain on paper towels.

8. **Serve** with the tabbouleh and yogurt.

wheat berries
with zucchini & parmesan

A wheat berry is a whole wheat kernel from which only the hull has been removed. It is composed of the bran, germ, and endosperm. They are extremely nutritious and deliciously crunchy.

Serves 4-6

20 minutes

12 hours

1 hour

1

2	cups (350 g) wheat berries
4	zucchini (courgettes), thinly sliced lengthwise
	Salt and freshly ground black pepper
6	tablespoons (90 ml) extra-virgin olive oil
2	tablespoons finely chopped fresh parsley
1	tablespoon finely chopped fresh mint + extra leaves, to garnish
1	tablespoon freshly squeezed lemon juice
20	walnuts, toasted and chopped
3	ounces (100 g) Parmesan cheese, shaved

1. **Soak** the wheat berries in cold water for 12 hours.

2. **Drain** and transfer to a large saucepan. Pour in enough hot water to cover the wheat and double the volume.

3. **Bring** to a boil and simmer until tender, about 1 hour.

4. **Grill** the zucchini in a hot grill pan until tender. Transfer to a bowl, season with salt and pepper, and drizzle with 2 tablespoons of oil. Sprinkle with the parsley and mint.

5. **Drain** the wheat berries thoroughly and set aside. Let cool.

6. **Place** the zucchini on a large serving dish and spoon the wheat over the top. Drizzle with the remaining oil and the lemon juice.

7. **Add** the toasted walnuts, Parmesan, and a few more leaves of fresh mint to garnish.

If you liked this recipe, you will love these as well.

bulgur with walnuts

98

spiced couscous with mushrooms

104

couscous with roasted vegetables

106

spiced couscous with mushrooms

Many types of couscous are served in Africa and the Middle East. In North America and Europe a quick-cooking version of the North African variety, made from semolina, is primarily served.

Serves 6

15 minutes

10 minutes

1

1⅓	cups (350 ml) water
5	tablespoons (75 ml) extra-virgin olive oil
	Salt
2	cups (350 g) couscous
1	tablespoon cumin seeds
2	cloves garlic, finely chopped
8	ounces (250 g) mushrooms, thinly sliced

12	cherry tomatoes, halved
3	ounces (100 g) Parmesan cheese, shaved
2	tablespoons finely chopped fresh marjoram
	Freshly ground black pepper
¼	cup (50 g) pine nuts, toasted

1. **Bring** the water to a boil in a large saucepan over medium heat.

2. **Add** 1 tablespoon of oil and salt to taste (about ½ teaspoon). Stir in the couscous and cumin and mix well.

3. **Remove** from the heat, cover, and let rest for 2 minutes.

4. **Add** the remaining 4 tablespoons of oil and return to the heat. Cook for 3 minutes, stirring constantly with a fork to separate the grains.

5. **Remove** from the heat and add the garlic, mushrooms, tomatoes, cheese, and marjoram. Season with salt and pepper. Sprinkle with the pine nuts.

6. **Serve** hot or at room temperature.

If you liked this recipe, you will love these as well.

wheat berries with zucchini & parmesan
102

couscous with roasted vegetables
106

bell peppers with mushroom couscous
238

couscous with roasted vegetables

Vary the vegetables you choose to roast according to what you like or have on hand.

- Serves 4
- 10 minutes
- 5 minutes
- 30–35 minutes
- 2

6	tablespoons (90 ml) extra-virgin olive oil
1	shallot, finely chopped
1	eggplant (aubergine), cut into small squares
2	zucchini (courgettes), cut into small cubes
1	large red bell pepper (capsicum), seeded and cut into small squares
1	large yellow bell pepper (capsicum), seeded and cut into small squares
¾	cup (75 g) pitted black olives
	Salt
1¼	cups (300 ml) water
1½	cups (270 g) couscous
2	tablespoons finely chopped fresh fennel leaves, to garnish (optional)

1. **Preheat** the oven to 400°F (200°C/gas 6). Heat 1 tablespoon of the oil in a small frying pan over medium heat. Add the shallot and sauté until softened, 3–4 minutes.

2. **Arrange** the eggplant, zucchini, bell peppers, and olives on a baking sheet. Add the shallot and drizzle with 3 tablespoons of oil.

3. **Bake** for 20–25 minutes, until the vegetables are tender and slightly charred. Season with salt.

4. **Bring** the water to a boil in a large saucepan over medium heat. Add 1 tablespoon of oil and salt to taste (about ½ teaspoon). Stir in the couscous and mix well.

5. **Remove** from the heat, cover, and let rest for 5 minutes.

6. **Add** the remaining 1 tablespoon of oil and return to the heat. Cook for 3 minutes, stirring constantly with a fork to separate the grains.

7. **Stir** in the roasted vegetables, and garnish with the fennel, if using.

8. **Serve** warm.

If you liked this recipe, you will love these as well.

falafel with tabbouleh
100

spiced couscous with mushrooms
104

roasted bell peppers with mushroom couscous
238

rice with tomato pesto
& mozzarella

This tasty tomato and rice dish makes a perfect lunch dish.

- Serves 4
- 10 minutes
- 15 minutes

- 1

12	sun-dried tomatoes packed in oil, drained
¼	cup (30 g) freshly grated Parmesan cheese
2	tablespoons blanched almonds, toasted
1	tablespoon salt-cured capers, rinsed and drained
¼	cup (60 ml) extra-virgin olive oil

	Freshly squeezed juice of ½ lemon
1½	cups (300 g) long-grain rice
	Salt and freshly ground black pepper
2	cups (100 g) arugula (rocket)
6	ounces (180 g) mini mozzarella balls

1. **Combine** the sun-dried tomatoes, cheese, almonds, capers, oil, and lemon juice in a food processor. Process until smooth.

2. **Bring** a large pot of salted water to a boil, add the rice, and boil until tender.

3. **Drain** well and transfer to a large bowl. Stir in the tomato pesto and season with salt and pepper.

4. **Arrange** the arugula on four serving dishes and top with the rice. Place the mozzarella balls on top, and serve hot.

If you liked this recipe, you will love these as well.

rice with feta & fresh herbs

110

tomato rice with cumin

112

aromatic lemon rice

114

rice with feta & fresh herbs

Use a short-grain, Mediterranean-style rice for best results with this recipe.

Serves 4

10 minutes

15 minutes

1

1	cup (50 g) mixed fresh herbs (such as marjoram, parsley, cilantro/coriander, thyme, chives, basil)	
2	tablespoons pine nuts	
8	walnuts, blanched	
1	fresh red chili, seeded and finely chopped (optional)	
1	clove garlic, peeled	

¼ cup (60 ml) extra-virgin olive oil
1 pound (500 g) cherry tomatoes, quartered
Salt
1½ cups (300 g) short-grain rice
3½ ounces (100 g) feta cheese, cut into small cubes

1. **Combine** the herbs in a food processor with the pine nuts, walnuts, chili, if using, and garlic. Process until just smooth, 10–15 seconds.

2. **Transfer** the mixture to a large bowl and stir in the oil.

3. **Add** the cherry tomatoes and season with salt.

4. **Bring** a large pot of salted water to a boil, add the rice, and simmer until tender.

5. **Drain** well and let cool for 2–3 minutes before adding to the bowl with the tomato-and-herb mixture.

6. **Add** the feta and toss well. Serve immediately.

If you liked this recipe, you will love these as well.

rice with tomato pesto & mozzarella

108

tomato rice with cumin

112

aromatic lemon rice

114

cumin rice with tomatoes

If preferred, you can also use ground cumin for this recipe.

Serves 4

10 minutes

20 minutes

1

3	tablespoons extra-virgin olive oil
1	large onion, finely chopped
1	teaspoon cumin seeds
1	clove garlic, finely chopped
6	medium tomatoes, peeled and chopped
1½	cups (300 g) long-grain rice
4	cups (1 liter) boiling water
2	tablespoons finely chopped fresh parsley, + extra sprigs to garnish
	Salt and freshly ground black pepper
1	tomato, thinly sliced, to garnish

1. **Heat** the oil in a large saucepan over low heat. Add the onion, cumin seeds, and garlic and sauté until the garlic turns pale gold, 3–4 minutes.

2. **Add** the chopped tomatoes.

3. **Stir** in the rice and pour in the water. Bring to a boil. Cover and simmer, stirring occasionally, until the rice is tender and has absorbed all of the liquid, 10–15 minutes.

4. **Add** the parsley and season with salt and pepper. Garnish with slices of tomato and the sprigs of parsley.

5. **Serve** hot.

If you liked this recipe, you will love these as well.

rice with **tomato pesto** & mozzarella

108

rice with **feta** & fresh herbs

110

roasted vegetables stuffed with rice

250

aromatic lemon rice

This rice dish goes very well with a vegetarian stew or curry.

Serves 4-6

20 minutes

20 minutes

2

2	cups (400 g) basmati rice
3	cups (750 ml) water
1	teaspoon ground turmeric
	Salt
4	tablespoons shredded (desiccated) coconut
¼	cup (60 ml) coconut milk
¼	cup (60 g) butter
¼	cup (60 ml) peanut oil
1	green chili, seeded and thinly sliced

	Seeds from 6 cardamom pods
3	whole black peppercorns
4	tablespoons chopped almonds
1	teaspoon cumin seeds
1	teaspoon mustard seeds
	Freshly squeezed juice of 1 lemon
	Fresh cilantro (coriander), to garnish

1. **Combine** the rice in a large saucepan with the water, turmeric, and salt. Bring to a boil, cover, and simmer over low heat for 10 minutes.

2. **Remove** from the heat and leave covered.

3. **Combine** the coconut with the coconut milk in a small bowl.

4. **Melt** the butter in a small saucepan over medium heat. Add the oil, chili, cardamom, peppercorns, almonds, cumin, and mustard seeds. Sauté until the mustard seeds begin to crackle, 3-4 minutes.

5. **Add** this mixture to the rice.

6. **Add** the lemon juice and coconut mixture and mix with a fork. Simmer over low heat until the rice is soft and fluffy, about 5 minutes.

7. **Serve** hot, garnished with the cilantro.

If you liked this recipe, you will love these as well.

rice with feta & fresh herns

110

tomato rice with cumin

112

champagne risotto with cilantro

116

champagne risotto with cilantro

Be sure to choose an Italian risotto rice. Arborio, Carnaroli, or Vialone Nano are all good choices.

Serves 4

10 minutes

25–30 minutes

1

4	tablespoons (60 g) butter	
1	large onion, finely chopped	
1¾	cups (350 g) risotto rice, such as Arborio	
1	cup (250 ml) dry champagne	
3	cups (750 ml) vegetable stock, boiling	

Salt and freshly ground black pepper

2 tablespoons finely chopped fresh cilantro (coriander)

3 ounces (90 g) Parmesan cheese, shaved

1. **Melt** 2 tablespoons of the butter in a large frying pan over medium heat. Add the onion and sauté until transparent, about 3 minutes.

2. **Add** the rice and sauté for 2 minutes.

3. **Pour** in the champagne and cook until it evaporates, about 5 minutes.

4. **Begin** adding the stock, a ladleful at a time, cooking and stirring until each addition has been absorbed and the rice is tender, 15–18 minutes.

5. **Season** with salt and pepper and mix well. Remove from the heat. Stir in the remaining 2 tablespoons butter. Cover and let rest for 1 minute.

6. **Sprinkle** with cilantro and Parmesan and serve hot.

If you liked this recipe, you will love these as well.

gorgonzola & cilantro risotto

118

zucchini & apple risotto

120

risotto with red roses

122

gorgonzola & cilantro risotto

If preferred, use another local blue cheese, such as Danish blue, Roquefort, or Stilton.

Serves 4

10 minutes

20–25 minutes

1

2	tablespoons butter
1	large onion, finely chopped
1½	cups (300 g) risotto rice, such as Arborio
⅓	cup (90 ml) dry white wine
4	cups (1 liter) vegetable stock, boiling

4	ounces (120 g) Gorgonzola cheese, cut into cubes
2	tablespoons finely chopped fresh cilantro (coriander)

1. **Melt** the butter in a large frying pan over medium heat.

2. **Add** the onion and sauté until softened, 3–4 minutes.

3. **Add** the rice and cook for 2 minutes, stirring constantly.

4. **Stir** in the wine and, when this has been absorbed, begin stirring in the stock a ladleful at a time. Cook and stir until each addition has been absorbed and the rice is tender, 15–18 minutes.

5. **Stir** in the Gorgonzola. Sprinkle with the cilantro, and serve hot.

If you liked this recipe, you will love these as well.

champagne risotto with cilantro

116

zucchini & apple risotto

120

risotto with red roses

122

zucchini & apple risotto

If using organic apples, leave the bright green skins on; this will make the finished dish more attractive.

Serves 4–6

10 minutes

20–25 minutes

1

2	green apples, such as Granny Smiths, peeled, cored, and cut into small cubes
	Freshly squeezed juice of 1 lemon
2	tablespoons extra-virgin olive oil
1	large onion, finely chopped
4	potatoes, peeled and cut into small cubes
3	zucchini (courgettes), cut into small cubes
1	carrot, peeled and cut into small cubes
1½	cups (350 g) risotto rice, such as Arborio
4	cups (1 liter) vegetable stock, boiling, with a pinch of saffron threads
1	teaspoon dark soy sauce
1	teaspoon curry powder
2	tablespoons finely chopped fresh dill + extra, to garnish
	Salt and freshly ground black pepper

1. **Put** the apples in a bowl. Drizzle with the lemon juice.

2. **Heat** the oil in a large frying pan over medium heat. Add the onion and sauté until softened, 3–4 minutes.

3. **Add** the potatoes, zucchini, and carrot and sauté for 2 minutes.

4. **Add** the rice and pour in a ladleful of the stock, stirring until it is absorbed. Add the apples and lemon juice and mix well. Keep adding the stock, a ladleful at a time, cooking and stirring until each addition has been absorbed and the rice is tender, 15–18 minutes.

5. **Remove** from the heat and stir in the soy sauce, curry powder, and dill. Season with salt and pepper and mix gently.

6. **Cover** and let rest for 1 minute. Garnish with dill, and serve hot.

If you liked this recipe, you will love these as well.

gorgonzola & cilantro risotto

118

vegetarian paella

124

nasi goreng

126

risotto with red roses

Many flowers can be eaten and they add a dash of exotic color. However, before adding them to food make sure they are clearly marked as edible. If getting them from your own garden, be sure they haven't been sprayed with pesticides or herbicides.

Serves 4

20 minutes

25–30 minutes

2

4	red roses (freshly opened buds)
½	cup (125 g) butter
2	cups (400 g) risotto rice, such as Arborio
⅛	teaspoon freshly grated nutmeg
	Freshly ground black pepper
½	cup (125 ml) dry white wine
4	cups (1 liter) vegetable stock, boiling
⅓	cup (90 ml) light (single) cream
4	ounces (125 g) Emmental cheese
	Few drops rosewater

1. **Pull** the petals off the roses, reserving 8 of the best to use as a garnish. (Keep in a bowl of cold water). Separate the brightly colored petals from the less brightly colored ones.

2. **Melt** half the butter in a large frying pan over medium heat and cook the less highly colored petals until wilted.

3. **Add** the rice and cook for 2 minutes, stirring constantly.

4. **Season** with nutmeg and pepper. Add the wine and cook until evaporated.

5. **Stir** in a ladleful of stock and cook, stirring often, until the stock is absorbed.

6. **Continue** adding the stock, a ladleful at a time, stirring often until each addition is absorbed and the rice is tender, 15–18 minutes.

7. **When** the rice is cooked, add the brightly colored rose petals. Fold in the cream and remaining butter. Add the Emmental and rosewater.

8. **Garnish** with the reserved petals. Serve hot.

If you liked this recipe, you will love these as well.

champagne risotto with cilantro

116

gorgonzola & cilantro risotto

118

zucchini & apple risotto

120

vegetarian paella

Traditionally made with seafood, or a mixture of seafood, chorizo, and vegetables, paella is a Spanish dish from the Valencia region. The recipe can easily be adapted to suit a vegetarian diet.

Serves 4

30 minutes

10 minutes

50–55 minutes

2

3	tablespoons extra-virgin olive oil
2	onions, sliced
3	garlic cloves, minced
2	red bell peppers (capsicums), seeded and sliced
6	tomatoes, quartered
2	cups (400 g) medium-grain rice, such as Goya or Arborio
5	ounces (150 g) green beans, chopped
2	zucchini (courgettes), sliced

1	teaspoon saffron threads mixed with 3 tablespoons hot water
1	tablespoon smoked paprika (pimentòn)
5	cups (1.25 liters) vegetable broth, hot
½	cup (75 g) frozen peas
1	cup (50 g) baby spinach leaves
¼	cup chopped fresh flat-leaf parsley
	Salt and freshly ground black pepper

1. **Heat** the oil in a large paella pan or skillet over medium-low heat. Add the onions and garlic and sauté until softened, 3–4 minutes.

2. **Add** the bell peppers and tomatoes and cook until softened, 5–7 minutes.

3. **Add** the rice, green beans, zucchini, saffron mixture, and paprika and stir to coat. Pour in the hot vegetable broth, decrease the heat to low, and gently simmer for 30 minutes, stirring occasionally to ensure even cooking of the rice.

4. **Stir** in the peas and spinach. Remove from the heat, cover with a lid or piece of aluminum foil, and set aside for 10 minutes to finish cooking. Add the parsley and season with salt and pepper.

5. **Serve** hot.

If you liked this recipe, you will love these as well.

rice with feta & fresh herbs

110

zucchini & apple risotto

120

nasi goreng

126

nasi goreng

Nasi goreng is a traditional dish from Indonesia and Malaysia and its name means quite literally "fried rice." Kecap manis is a sweet Indonesian variety of soy sauce. Replace with ordinary soy sauce if you can't get it.

Serves 4

20 minutes

3 hours

20 minutes

2

2	cups (400 g) long-grain rice
3	cups (750 ml) water
4	tablespoons (60 ml) peanut oil
2	large eggs, beaten
1	small onion, sliced
2	garlic cloves, minced
1	teaspoon finely chopped fresh ginger
1	green chili, seeded and finely chopped

1	tablespoon tamarind paste
1	red bell pepper (capsicum), seeded and thinly sliced
$1/4$	Chinese cabbage (wom bok), shredded
2	cups (100 g) bean sprouts
1	tablespoon soy sauce
1	tablespoon kecap manis
4	scallions (spring onions), thinly sliced

1. **Put** the rice in a bowl and cover with cold water. Let soak for 1 hour. Rinse under cold running water until the water runs clear.

2. **Put** the rice and water in a pot and bring to a boil. Cover and simmer over low heat until tender and the liquid has been absorbed, 20–25 minutes. Spread the rice onto two baking sheets and let cool for 2 hours.

3. **Heat** 2 tablespoons of oil in a large wok over medium heat. Add the egg and cook for 1–2 minutes on each side to make a thin omelet. Transfer to a

cutting board, roll up, and cut into thin strips.

4. **Heat** the remaining oil in the wok over medium heat. Add the onion, garlic, ginger, and chili and stir-fry until softened, 3–4 minutes.

5. **Add** the tamarind and peppers and stir-fry until tender, 3–4 minutes. Add the cabbage, rice, bean sprouts, soy sauce, and kecap manis and stir-fry until hot, 2–3 minutes.

6. **Serve** hot, with the omelet and scallions.

If you liked this recipe, you will love these as well.

gorgonzola & cilantro risotto

118

zucchini & apple risotto

120

risotto with red roses

122

baked polenta
with tasty tomato topping

Polenta is a traditional northern Italian dish made by stirring yellow cornmeal and water over low heat until thickened and creamy.

Serves 6

20 minutes

1 hour

1 hour

2

BASIC POLENTA

8 cups (2 liters) water
2 cups (300 g) coarse-grained polenta (yellow cornmeal)

TOMATO TOPPING

¼ cup (60 ml) extra-virgin olive oil

4 cloves garlic, finely chopped
2 (14-ounce/400-g) cans tomatoes, with juice
  Salt and freshly ground black pepper
1 cup (120 g) freshly grated Parmesan cheese

1. **To prepare the basic polenta,** bring the water to a boil in a large pot.

2. **Gradually** sprinkle in the polenta, stirring constantly. Continue cooking over low heat, stirring often, until the polenta comes away from the sides of the pan, 45–50 minutes.

3. **Drizzle** cold water over a large metal pan. Spread the polenta to ½ inch (1 cm) thick. Set aside to cool for and harden at least 1 hour.

4. **To prepare the tomato topping,** preheat the oven to 400°F (200°C/gas 6).

5. **Lightly** oil a large baking dish. Heat the oil in a large frying pan over medium heat. Add the garlic and sauté until pale gold, 3–4 minutes.

6. **Add** the tomatoes and simmer until reduced, 15–20 minutes. Season with salt and pepper.

7. **Use** a glass or cookie cutter to cut out disks of polenta about 2 inches (5 cm) in diameter. Arrange in the baking dish, overlapping slightly.

8. **Cover** with sauce and sprinkle with the Parmesan.

9. **Bake** for 10–15 minutes, until the cheese has melted.

If you liked this recipe, you will love these as well.

cumin rice with tomatoes

112

baked polenta in cheese sauce

130

polenta with mushrooms

132

baked polenta
in cheese sauce

This hearty dish is perfect for cold winter evenings. Serve with a green or mixed salad for a complete and nourishing meal.

Serves 6

20 minutes

3 hours

65–75 minutes

2

1	recipe basic polenta (see page 128)
2	tablespoons butter
1	tablespoon all-purpose (plain) flour
1	cup (250 ml) milk
	Pinch of nutmeg

6	ounces (180 g) Gorgonzola cheese, chopped
6	ounces (180 g) Emmental (or Gruyère, or similar) cheese, thinly sliced
½	cup (60 g) freshly grated Parmesan cheese

1. **Prepare** the polenta. When cooked, turn out onto a metal pan and spread to 1 inch (2.5 cm) thick. Let cool for 3 hours.

2. **Melt** the butter in a saucepan over low heat. When it stops bubbling, add the flour and cook over low heat for 1–2 minutes, stirring constantly.

3. **Begin** adding the milk, a little at a time, stirring until the sauce is smooth. Season with a little nutmeg.

4. **Turn up** the heat and add all three cheeses, a handful at a time, stirring until smooth.

5. **Preheat** the oven to 400°F (200°C/gas 6). Oil a baking dish large enough to hold the polenta and sauce in a double layer.

6. **Cut** the polenta into 1-inch (2.5-cm) cubes.

7. **Cover** the bottom of the dish with half the polenta and pour half the sauce over the top. Put the remaining polenta on top and cover with the remaining sauce.

8. **Bake** for 25–30 minutes, until the top is golden brown. Serve hot.

If you liked this recipe, you will love these as well.

gorgonzola & cilantro risotto

118

baked polenta with tasty tomato topping

128

polenta with mushrooms

132

polenta with mushrooms

If you can get them, use porcini mushrooms (boletus edulis) for a superb meal. Serve with a glass of good red wine.

- Serves 4–6
- 30 minutes
- 45–50 minutes

- 2

1	recipe basic polenta (see page 128)

MUSHROOM SAUCE

2	pounds (1 kg) chanterelle or white mushrooms
¼	cup (60 ml) extra-virgin olive oil
2	cloves garlic, finely chopped
1	large red onion, finely chopped
	Salt and freshly ground black pepper
2	tablespoons finely chopped fresh parsley
⅓	cup (75 g) shaved Parmesan cheese

1. **Prepare** the polenta.

2. **To prepare the mushroom sauce,** while the polenta is cooking,, chop the mushroom stems into cubes. Cut the largest ones in half, leaving the smaller ones whole.

3. **Heat** the oil in a large frying pan over medium heat. Add the garlic and onion and sauté until softened, 3–4 minutes.

4. **Add** the mushrooms and season with salt and pepper. Cover and simmer over low heat for 20 minutes, stirring often. Add the parsley.

5. **Spoon** the hot polenta onto individual serving plates. Spoon the mushrooms with their cooking juices on top and garnish with the Parmesan.

6. **Serve** immediately.

If you liked this recipe, you will love these as well.

spiced **couscous** with mushrooms

104

baked **polenta** with tasty tomato topping

128

baked **polenta** in cheese sauce

130

pasta
& gnocchi

rigatoni with roasted bell pepper sauce

If you are pushed for time you could use a 12-ounce (350-g) jar of roasted bell peppers preserved in oil. Drain well, coarsely chop, and toss with the pasta and cheese.

- Serves 4–6
- 30 minutes
- 50–60 minutes
- 2

2	large red bell peppers (capsicums)
¼	cup (60 ml) extra-virgin olive oil
1½	pounds (750 g) tomatoes, peeled and sliced
2	cloves garlic, finely chopped
2	tablespoons finely chopped fresh parsley

	Salt and freshly ground black pepper
1	pound (500 g) rigatoni
6	tablespoons freshly grated pecorino cheese

1. **Broil** (grill) the bell peppers whole until their skins are blackened, turning frequently. Put the blackened bell peppers in a plastic bag and set aside for 10 minutes. Remove from the bag and discard the skins and seeds. Wipe clean with paper towels. Chop the flesh into small strips.

2. **Heat** the oil in a large frying pan over medium heat. Add the tomatoes, garlic, and parsley. Season with salt and pepper and simmer over low heat for 20–30 minutes.

3. **Meanwhile**, cook the rigatoni in a large pan of salted boiling water until al dente. Drain the pasta and add to the pan with the sauce.

4. **Add** the bell peppers and pecorino and stir gently.

5. **Serve** hot.

If you liked this recipe, you will love these as well.

rigatoni with cauliflower

138

fusilli with mushrooms

140

farfalle with yogurt & avocado

144

rigatoni with cauliflower

Penne or farfalle would also be good with this sauce.

- Serves 4–6
- 15 minutes
- 15 minutes

- 1

1	small cauliflower, broken into florets
1/3	cup (90 ml) extra-virgin olive oil
1	large white onion, finely chopped
	Salt and freshly ground black pepper
1/4	teaspoon saffron threads

2	tablespoons water
6	anchovy fillets
1/3	cup (50 g) raisins
1/2	cup (60 g) pine nuts
1	pound (500 g) rigatoni
1	tablespoon finely chopped fresh basil + extra to garnish
1/2	cup (60 g) freshly grated pecorino cheese

1. **Cook** the cauliflower in a large pan of salted boiling water until crunchy tender, 2–3 minutes. Remove the cauliflower with a slotted spoon, reserving the water.

2. **Heat** half the oil in a large saucepan over medium heat. Add the onion and sauté until pale gold, about 5 minutes. Season with salt and pepper.

3. **Add** the saffron and water and stir well. Add the cauliflower, cover, and simmer over very low heat.

4. **Heat** the remaining oil in a small pot. Add the anchovies and stir until dissolved into the oil.

5. **Add** the anchovy mixture to the pan with the cauliflower together with the raisins and pine nuts.

6. **Meanwhile**, cook the rigatoni in the water used to cook the cauliflower, until al dente.

7. **Drain** the pasta and add to the pan with the sauce. Stir in the basil and cheese. Toss gently, garnish with extra basil, and serve hot.

If you liked this recipe, you will love these as well.

rigatoni with roasted bell peper sauce
136

fusilli with mushrooms
140

farfalle with radicchio & goat cheese
142

fusilli with mushrooms

If liked, replace the white mushrooms with the same weight of mixed wild mushrooms.

- Serves 4–6
- 15 minutes
- 30 minutes
- 1

4	tablespoons extra-virgin olive oil
4	cloves garlic, finely chopped
1½	pounds (750 g) white mushrooms, trimmed and thickly sliced
5	tablespoons finely chopped fresh parsley
	Salt and freshly ground black pepper
1	pound (500 g) fusilli or rotini

1. **Heat** 2 tablespoons of the oil in a large frying pan over medium heat. Add 3 cloves of garlic and sauté until pale gold, 2–3 minutes.

2. **Add** the mushrooms and half the parsley, season with salt and pepper, and simmer until the mushrooms are tender and their juices have reduced, 10–15 minutes.

3. **Meanwhile**, cook the pasta in a large pot of salted boiling water until al dente. Drain well and add to the pan with the sauce.

4. **Sprinkle** with the remaining garlic and parsley and drizzle with the remaining 2 tablespoons oil. Toss for 1–2 minutes, and serve hot.

If you liked this recipe, you will love these as well.

rigatoni with cauliflower

138

spicy fusilli with eggplant

146

linguine with mushrooms

150

farfalle with radicchio & goat cheese

Red radicchio, also known as Italian chicory, has a bitter, slightly spicy taste which mellows when it is grilled or sautéed.

- Serves 4-6
- 10 minutes
- 20 minutes

- 1

1	pound (500 g) farfalle
4	tablespoons extra-virgin olive oil
1	large red onion, thinly sliced
2	heads red radicchio, cut into strips

	Salt and freshly ground black pepper
¼	cup (60 ml) beer
5	ounces (150 g) chèvre or other soft fresh goat cheese
2	tablespoons milk

1. **Cook** the pasta in a large pot of salted boiling water until it is al dente.

2. **Meanwhile**, heat 3 tablespoons of the oil in a large frying pan over medium heat. Add the onion and sauté until softened, about 3 minutes.

3. **Add** the radicchio and season with salt and pepper. Sauté for a few minutes, then add the beer. When the beer has evaporated, add the goat cheese and stir well, softening the mixture with the milk.

4. **Drain** the pasta well and add to the pan with the sauce. Toss for 1–2 minutes over medium heat.

5. **Drizzle** with the remaining 1 tablespoon oil, and serve hot.

If you liked this recipe, you will love these as well.

fusilli with mushrooms

140

farfalle with yogurt & avocado

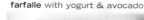

144

spicy fusilli with eggplant

146

farfalle with yogurt & avocado

Serve this unusual pasta dish during the summer when its refreshing flavors will be most appreciated.

 Serves 4-6

30 minutes

20 minutes

1

4	tablespoons (60 ml) extra-virgin olive oil
1	large onion, chopped
2	cloves garlic, finely chopped
1	tablespoon dry white wine
1	pound (500 g) farfalle
2	ripe avocados
	Freshly squeezed juice of 1 lemon

1	cup (250 ml) plain yogurt
	Salt and freshly ground black pepper
1	fresh red chili, thinly sliced
1	celery heart, thinly sliced
2	tablespoons salt-cured capers, rinsed
2	tablespoons finely chopped fresh parsley

1. **Heat** 2 tablespoons of the oil in a large frying pan over medium heat. Add the onion and garlic and sauté until softened, 3–4 minutes.

2. **Add** the wine and simmer until evaporated. Set aside.

3. **Cook** the pasta in a large pot of salted boiling water until al dente.

4. **Peel**, pit, and dice the avocado. Drizzle with the lemon juice to keep it from turning brown.

5. **Whisk** the yogurt with the remaining 2 tablespoons of oil in a large bowl.

6. **Season** with salt and pepper. Add the chili, celery, capers, and parsley.

7. **Drain** the pasta and toss in the yogurt sauce. Add the onion and avocado, toss again, and serve hot.

If you liked this recipe, you will love these as well.

rigatoni with cauliflower

138

fusilli with mushrooms

140

fresh pasta with scallions & tomatoes

156

spicy fusilli with eggplant

Eggplant, also known as aubergines, are a healthy food choice. They contain plenty of heart-healthy dietary fiber as well as a range of antioxidants.

Serves 4-6

15 minutes

20 minutes

1

⅓	cup (90 ml) extra-virgin olive oil	
2	cloves garlic, finely chopped	
1	large eggplant (aubergine), cut into small cubes	
1	fresh chili, seeded and finely chopped	
	Salt and freshly ground black pepper	

1	pound (500 g) fusilli, rotini, or other short pasta
2	tablespoons salted capers, rinsed
2	tablespoons finely chopped fresh oregano
4	tablespoons pine nuts

1. **Heat** the oil in a large frying pan over medium heat. Add the garlic and sauté until softened, 3–4 minutes.

2. **Add** the eggplant and chili and simmer for 10 minutes, stirring often. Season with salt and pepper.

3. **Meanwhile,** cook the pasta in a large pot of salted boiling water until al dente.

4. **Drain** the pasta thoroughly and place in the pan with the eggplant. Add the capers, oregano, and pine nuts. Toss well, and serve hot.

If you liked this recipe, you will love these as well.

fusilli with mushrooms

140

farfalle with radicchio & goat cheese

144

farfalle with radicchio & goat cheese

142

spicy spaghetti with garlic, pine nuts & raisins

This unusual recipe comes from Florence, where it is traditionally served on 24 June to celebrate San Giovanni, the city's patron saint.

Serves 4–6

10 minutes

15 minutes

1

1	pound (500 g) spaghetti
1/3	cup (90 ml) extra-virgin olive oil
4	cloves garlic, finely chopped
1	fresh red chile, seeded and finely chopped
3/4	cup (100 g) pine nuts

1/2	cup (90 g) golden raisins (sultanas)
	Salt and freshly ground black pepper
5	tablespoons finely chopped fresh parsley

1. **Cook** the pasta in a large pot of salted boiling water until al dente.

2. **While** the pasta is cooking, heat the oil in a large frying pan over medium heat. Add the garlic and chile and sauté until the garlic turns pale gold, 3–4 minutes.

3. **Add** the pine nuts and golden raisins. Season with salt and pepper. Sauté for 1 minute more.

4. **Drain** the pasta and add to the pan with the sauce. Add the parsley and toss over high heat for 1 minute.

5. **Serve** hot.

If you liked this recipe, you will love these as well.

rigatoni with cauliflower

138

linguine with mushrooms

150

spaghetti with fresh tomato sauce & lemon

154

linguine with mushrooms

Replace the chili in this recipe with 1 teaspoon of red pepper flakes. Use more or less chili or pepper flakes according to how spicy you like your food.

Serves 4–6

30 minutes

40 minutes

1

1½	pounds (750 g) mixed mushrooms (porcini, white button mushrooms, chanterelle, enoki)
1	small onion, finely chopped
¼	cup (60 ml) extra-virgin olive oil
	Salt
2	cloves garlic, finely chopped

1	small dried chili, crumbled
¼	cup (60 ml) dry white wine
20	cherry tomatoes, quartered
	Leaves from 1 bunch fresh basil, torn
1	tablespoon finely chopped fresh parsley
1	pound (500 g) linguine

1. **Clean** the mushrooms very carefully and cut the larger ones into small pieces.

2. **Heat** the oil in a frying pan over low heat. Add the onion, cover, and sweat for 20 minutes. Season with salt and add the garlic and chili.

3. **Increase** the heat and pour in the wine. Add the mushrooms and simmer over high heat until the wine has evaporated.

4. **Stir** in the tomatoes, basil, and parsley, and simmer until the mushrooms are tender, about 10 minutes. Season with salt.

5. **Meanwhile,** cook the pasta in a large pot of salted boiling water until al dente.

6. **Drain** and add to the sauce. Toss well and serve hot.

If you liked this recipe, you will love these as well.

fusilli with mushrooms

140

spicy spaghetti with garlic, pine nuts & raisins

148

spaghetti with fresh tomato sauce & lemon

154

whole-wheat spaghetti with pesto, potatoes & beans

This recipe comes from the city of Genoa, in the northwest of Italy. With its mild seaside climate, Genoa has ideal weather for growing fresh basil and it is the hometown of pesto.

Serves 4–6

25 minutes

15 minutes

1

PESTO

1	large bunch fresh basil leaves
2	cloves garlic
2	tablespoons pine nuts
½	cup (125 ml) extra-virgin olive oil
4	tablespoons freshly grated pecorino cheese
	Salt and freshly ground black pepper

PASTA

12	ounces (350 g) green beans, cut into short lengths
1	pound (500 g) whole-wheat (wholemeal) spaghetti
8	new potatoes, cut into small cubes
	Freshly ground black pepper

1. **To prepare the pesto,** combine the basil, garlic, and pine nuts in a food processor and process until finely chopped, gradually adding the oil as you chop. Transfer to a small bowl. Stir in the cheese, and season with salt and pepper.

2. **To prepare the pasta,** cook the green beans in a large pot of salted boiling water until almost tender, 4–5 minutes. Drain and set aside.

3. **Cook** the pasta in a large pot of salted boiling water for 5 minutes. Add the potatoes and cook until the pasta is al dente and the potatoes are tender, 7–8 minutes more.

4. **Drain** well, reserving 2 tablespoons of the cooking liquid. Put the pasta and potatoes in a heated serving bowl.

5. **Stir** the reserved cooking liquid into the pesto. Pour the pesto into the pasta and potatoes, add the green beans, and toss well.

6. **Season** with pepper. Serve hot.

If you liked this recipe, you will love these as well.

spicy spaghetti with garlic, pine nuts & raisins

148

linguine with mushrooms

150

spaghetti with fresh tomato sauce & lemon

154

spaghetti with fresh tomato sauce & lemon

This sauce is best served during the summer months when fresh, locally-grown tomatoes are at their succulent best.

- Serves 4–6
- 10 minutes
- 15 minutes

1

2	pounds (1 kg) ripe tomatoes	Freshly squeezed juice of 1 lemon
1	pound (500 g) spaghetti	
4	tablespoons finely chopped fresh basil + extra leaves to garnish	2 cloves garlic, finely chopped
⅓	cup (90 ml) extra-virgin olive oil	Salt and freshly ground black pepper

1. **Blanch** the tomatoes in boiling water for 2 minutes. Drain and peel them. Coarsely chop the flesh.

2. **Cook** the pasta in a large pot of salted boiling water until al dente.

3. **Drain** well and transfer to a large serving dish.

4. **Add** the tomatoes, basil, oil, lemon juice, and garlic. Season with salt and pepper. Toss well.

5. **Garnish** with basil and serve hot.

If you liked this recipe, you will love these as well.

linguine with mushrooms

150

whole-wheat spaghetti with pesto, potatoes & beans

152

spaghetti with fresh tomato sauce & lemon

154

fresh pasta
with scallions & tomatoes

Homemade fresh pasta is a true delicacy, but you will need a little time and practise to get it right.

- Serves 4
- 20 minutes
- 1 hour
- 30 minutes

- 3

3	cups (450 g) all-purpose (plain) flour
4	large eggs, lightly beaten
12	ounces (350 g) cherry tomatoes, halved
½	cup (75 g) freshly grated Parmesan cheese
	Salt and freshly ground black pepper
2	tablespoons finely chopped fresh thyme
⅓	cup (90 ml) extra-virgin olive oil
8	scallions (spring onions), trimmed and thinly sliced
1	cup (250 ml) plain yogurt, at room temperature

1. **To prepare the fresh pasta,** put the flour in a mound on a clean work surface. Make a well in the center and add the eggs. Use a fork to gradually incorporate the eggs into the flour. When almost all the flour has been absorbed, use your hands to gather the dough up into a ball.

2. **Knead** the dough by pushing down and forward on the ball of pasta with the palm of your hand. Fold the dough in half, give it a quarter-turn, and repeat. After 15–20 minutes, the dough should be smooth and silky, with tiny air bubbles visible near the surface.

3. **Wrap** in plastic wrap (cling film) and let rest at room temperature for 30 minutes.

4. **Roll** the dough through a pasta machine, reducing the thickness setting by one notch each time, until you reach the thinnest setting.

5. **Put** the pasta machine on the setting for tagliatelle or pappardelle and cut each sheet. Fold the pasta into "nests" and set aside until you are ready to cook.

6. **Preheat** the oven to 400°F (200°C/gas 6). Place the tomatoes cut side up in a baking dish. Sprinkle with half the Parmesan, salt, pepper, and thyme. Drizzle with half the oil. Bake for 15–20 minutes, until the cheese is browned.

7. **Heat** the remaining oil in a large frying pan over medium heat. Add the scallions and sauté until softened, 3–4 minutes. Season with salt and pepper and keep warm over very low heat.

8. **Cook** the pasta in a large pot of salted boiling water until al dente, 3–4 minutes.

9. **Remove** the scallion sauce from the heat and stir in the yogurt and remaining Parmesan.

10. **Drain** the pasta and add to the pan with the scallion and yogurt sauce. Toss gently. Add the baked tomatoes and toss again. Serve hot.

watercress tagliolini with pesto

This dish is packed with healthy vitamins and minerals.

 Serves 4

🕐 1 hour

🌡 1 hour

⏱ 4–6 minutes

🍴 3

8	ounces (250 g) watercress + extra to garnish
1 ½	cups (250 g) all-purpose (plain) flour
1 ½	cups (250 g) whole-wheat (wholemeal) flour
½	teaspoon salt

¾	cup (180 ml) water
1 ½	cups (75 g) fresh basil
¼	cup (60 ml) extra-virgin olive oil
3	ounces (90 g) cream cheese
4	tablespoons pine nuts
3	cloves garlic

1. **Cook** the watercress in salted boiling water until wilted, 2–3 minutes. Drain and finely chop in a food processor.

2. **Put** both flours and salt in a large bowl. Add the watercress and stir in the water until the dough is firm.

3. **Transfer** to a floured work surface and knead until smooth and elastic, about 10 minutes. Wrap in plastic wrap (cling film) and let rest for 1 hour.

4. **Roll** the dough through a pasta machine, reducing the thickness setting by one notch each time, until you reach the thinnest setting.

5. **Put** the pasta machine on the setting for tagliolini (thin ribbons) and cut each sheet. Fold into "nests." Combine the basil, oil, cream cheese, pine nuts, and garlic in a food processor and process until smooth.

6. **Cook** the tagliolini in a large pot of salted boiling water until al dente, 2–3 minutes.

7. **Drain** and spoon the sauce over the top. Serve garnished with extra watercress.

If you liked this recipe, you will love these as well.

fresh pasta with scallions & tomatoes
156

tagliatelle with walnut pesto
160

spinach gnocchi with tomato sauce
166

tagliatelle with walnut pesto

Walnuts are a very healthy food for vegetarians. They are rich in heart-healthy omega-3 fatty acids.

- Serves 4
- 30 minutes
- 1 hour
- 15 minutes

- 2

14	ounces (400 g) store-bought tagliatelle or fresh pasta (see page 156)
⅓	cup (45 g) pine nuts
1	pound (500 g) walnuts, in shell (or 1 cup/120 g shelled walnuts)
2	cloves garlic
1	cup (50 g) fresh parsley
¼	cup (60 ml) extra-virgin olive oil
	Salt

1. **If using homemade pasta**, prepare the pasta dough, let rest, then cut into tagliatelle. Fold into nests and set aside.

2. **Preheat** the oven to 350°F (180°C/gas 4).

3. **Roast** the pine nuts in a baking dish until pale gold, about 5 minutes. Shell the walnuts. Coarsely chop a few by hand to garnish. Finely chop the rest in a food processor with the pine nuts, garlic, parsley, and oil. Season with salt.

4. **Cook** the pasta in a large pot of salted boiling water until al dente, 3–4 minutes.

5. **Drain** and place in a heated serving dish. Cover with the sauce, toss carefully, garnish with the reserved walnuts, and serve.

If you liked this recipe, you will love these as well.

whole-wheat spaghetti with pesto, potatoes & beans

152

fresh pasta with scallions & tomatoes

156

spinach gnocchi with tomato sauce

158

potato gnocchi
with tomato & parmesan

Potato gnocchi are not difficult to make, and they are very versatile. Serve them with this classic tomato sauce, or try them with melted butter and fresh herbs (sage is very good), melted Gorgonzola, fresh cream, and plenty of freshly ground black pepper, or any of your other favorite pasta sauces.

Serves 4

20 minutes

1 hour

1 hour

2

POTATO GNOCCHI

2	pounds (1 kg) boiling potatoes, with skins
1²⁄₃	cups (250 g) all-purpose (plain) flour
½	teaspoon salt
1	large egg
3	tablespoons freshly grated Parmesan cheese

TOMATO SAUCE

3	tablespoons butter
2	pounds (1 kg) firm-ripe tomatoes, peeled and coarsely chopped
2	cloves garlic, lightly crushed but whole
1	red onion, thinly sliced
	Salt
¾	cup (90 g) freshly grated Parmesan cheese

1. **To prepare the potato gnocchi,** boil the potatoes in salted water until tender, 20–25 minutes. Slip off the skins, then mash with a potato masher until smooth (or run them through a potato ricer).

2. **Add** the flour, salt, egg, and Parmesan and knead until the dough is smooth. Shape into a ball.

3. **Break** off little bits of dough and roll them out into cylinders about as thick as your finger. Cut them into pieces about ¾ inch (2 cm) long. Set aside to dry on a clean cloth dusted with semolina for at least 1 hour before cooking.

4. **Preheat** the oven to 400°F (200°C/gas 6).

5. **To prepare the tomato sauce,** melt the butter in a medium saucepan over medium heat. Add the tomatoes, garlic, onion, and salt. Cover and simmer for about 10 minutes, until the tomatoes have broken down. Uncover and let reduce for 10 minutes.

6. **Remove** from the heat and process in a food processor until smooth.

7. **Cook** the gnocchi in small batches in a large pot of salted boiling water until they rise to the surface, about 2 minutes. Use a slotted spoon to remove the gnocchi and transfer to a baking dish.

8. **Cover** with some tomato sauce and sprinkle with some Parmesan. Repeat until all the gnocchi, sauce, and Parmesan are in the dish.

9. **Bake** for 12–15 minutes, or until bubbling and hot. Serve hot.

potato gnocchi with fresh herbs & sun-dried tomatoes

Pecorino is made from ewe's milk and adds a tasty flavor to this sauce. If preferred, use Parmesan cheese instead.

 Serves 4

⏱ 30 minutes

🌡 1 hour

⏲ 30 minutes

🍸 2

1 recipe potato gnocchi (see page 162) or 1 pound (500 g) store-bought fresh potato gnocchi

SAUCE

1¼ cups (150 g) freshly grated pecorino or Parmesan cheese

¾ cup (180 ml) milk

1 tablespoon cornstarch (cornflour)

4 tablespoons finely chopped fresh parsley

1 small bunch fresh chives, snipped

1 tablespoon finely chopped fresh thyme

1 tablespoon finely chopped fresh mint

Salt and freshly ground black pepper

16 sun-dried tomatoes packed in oil, drained and finely chopped

1. **If using** homemade potato gnocchi, prepare them first.

2. **To prepare the sauce,** combine the pecorino with ½ cup (120 ml) of the milk in a small saucepan over low heat.

3. **Put** the cornstarch in a small bowl and stir in the remaining ¼ cup (60 ml) of milk. Add to the pecorino, stirring constantly, and bring to a gentle simmer. Remove from the heat and stir in the herbs and sun-dried tomatoes. Season with salt and pepper.

4. **Cook** the gnocchi in small batches in a large pot of salted boiling water until they rise to the surface, about 2 minutes.

5. **Use** a slotted spoon to remove the gnocchi and transfer to a heated serving dish.

6. **Pour** the sauce over the top. Toss gently, and serve hot.

If you liked this recipe, you will love these as well.

potato gnocchi with tomato & parmesan
162

herb gnocchi
168

baked semolina gnocchi with parmesan
174

spinach gnocchi
with tomato sauce

These classic Italian spinach gnocchi are known as *ignudi* (nudes) in Tuscany, because they have the same ingredients as spinach and ricotta ravioli but lack the fresh pasta casings.

Serves 6

30 minutes

30 minutes

20 minutes

2

2	cups (500 g) fresh ricotta, strained through a fine-mesh sieve
1½	cups (350 g) finely chopped cooked spinach, well drained
2	large eggs
1	cup (120 g) freshly grated Parmesan cheese + extra to serve

½	cup (75 g) + 2 tablespoons all-purpose (plain) flour
	Salt and freshly ground black pepper
	Finely grated zest of ½ unwaxed lemon
1	recipe tomato sauce (see page 162)

1. **Mix** the ricotta and spinach in a large bowl.

2. **Add** the eggs, 1 cup (120 g) of Parmesan, and ½ cup (75 g) flour. Season with salt and pepper and add the lemon zest.

3. **Dip** your hands in the remaining 2 tablespoons of flour and form the spinach mixture into 2-inch (5-cm) balls. Set aside to rest for at least 30 minutes before cooking.

4. **Cook** the gnocchi in a large pot of salted boiling water until they rise to the surface, 3–4 minutes per batch.

5. **Remove** with a slotted spoon and transfer to individual serving dishes.

6. **Spoon** the tomato sauce over the top of each serving and sprinkle with the extra Parmesan cheese. Serve hot.

If you liked this recipe, you will love these as well.

potato gnocchi with fresh herbs & sun-dried tomatoes

164

herb gnocchi

168

carrot & potato gnocchi with arugula sauce

172

herb gnocchi

Twelve ounces (350 g) is a lot of herbs! You will need about seven packed cups of different herbs.

- 🍽 Serves 4
- 🕐 45 minutes
- 🔥 1 hour

- 🍴 2

12	ounces (350 g) mixed fresh herbs (mint, basil, fennel, sage, parsley, rosemary)
3	pounds (1.5 kg) boiling potatoes, with skins
¼	cup (60 ml) extra-virgin olive oil
	Salt and freshly ground white pepper
1	large egg, lightly beaten

1⅓	cups (200 g) all-purpose (plain) flour
2	tablespoons butter
½	onion, finely chopped
¼	cup (60 ml) dry white wine
1	clove garlic, finely chopped
	tablespoons freshly grated Parmesan or pecorino cheese

1. **Boil** the herbs in salted water until tender, 2–3 minutes. Drain, squeezing out excess moisture. Chop finely.

2. **Cook** the potatoes in salted boiling water until tender, 20–25 minutes. Drain and peel. Mash and place in a bowl to cool.

3. **Heat** the oil in a frying pan over medium heat. Add the herbs and sauté for 2 minutes.

4. **Season** the potatoes with salt and pepper and work in half the herbs, the egg, and 1 cup (150 g) flour. Break off walnut-size pieces of dough. Shape into balls. Coat with remaining flour.

5. **Melt** the butter in a frying pan over medium heat. Add the onion and sauté until softened, 3–4 minutes.

6. **Pour** in the wine and let evaporate. Add the garlic and remaining herbs and simmer for 10 minutes.

7. **Cook** the gnocchi in batches in salted boiling water until they rise to the surface, 3–4 minutes.

8. **Use** a slotted spoon to transfer to serving plates. Top with sauce and cheese.

If you liked this recipe, you will love these as well.

spinach gnocchi with tomato sauce
166

baked gnocchi with butter & sage
170

carrot & potato gnocchi with arugula sauce
172

baked gnocchi
with butter & sage

The simple sage and butter sauce is all that is needed to set off the delicious flavors of the swiss chard gnocchi.

Serves 6

50 minutes

45 minutes

2

12	ounces (350 g) Swiss chard (silverbeet)
$3\frac{1}{2}$	cups (400 g) day-old bread crumbs
2	cups (500 ml) milk
2	large egg yolks
6	tablespoons fine dry bread crumbs

$\frac{1}{8}$	teaspoon freshly grated nutmeg
	Salt and freshly ground black pepper
$\frac{3}{4}$	cup (90 g) freshly grated Parmesan cheese
$\frac{1}{2}$	cup (125 g) butter
	Fresh sage leaves

1. **Preheat** the oven to 400°F (200°C/gas 6).

2. **Cook** the Swiss chard in a large pot of salted boiling water until tender, 7–10 minutes. Squeeze dry and finely chop.

3. **Butter** a large baking dish. Soak the bread in the milk for 15 minutes. Squeeze out excess milk and transfer to a food processor. Add the Swiss chard and egg yolks and process until smooth.

4. **Mix** in the fine dry bread crumbs, nutmeg, salt, and pepper. Break off walnut-size pieces and form into elongated $1\frac{1}{2}$-inch (4-cm) gnocchi.

5. **Cook** the gnocchi in batches in a large pot of salted boiling water until they rise to the surface, about 3 minutes.

6. **Use** a slotted spoon to scoop out and arrange in the dish.

7. **Sprinkle** with the Parmesan.

8. **Melt** the butter with the sage in a small saucepan and drizzle over the gnocchi. Season with salt. Bake for 10–15 minutes, until the cheese is bubbling.

9. **Serve** hot.

If you liked this recipe, you will love these as well.

spinach gnocchi with tomato sauce

166

herb gnocchi

168

baked semolina gnocchi with parmesan

174

carrot & potato gnocchi
with arugula sauce

Serve these delicately-flavored gnocchi on special occasions.

 Serves 6

35 minutes

1–2 hours

45 minutes

2

CARROT & POTATO GNOCCHI

2	pounds (1 kg) carrots, cut into thick rounds
1	pound (500 g) potatoes, peeled and cut into chunks
1	large egg, lightly beaten
1⅓	cups (200 g) all-purpose (plain) flour
	Salt and freshly ground white pepper
¼	teaspoon freshly grated nutmeg

ARUGULA SAUCE

2	cups (100 g) arugula (rocket)
2	cloves garlic
4	tablespoons pine nuts
⅔	cup (100 g) freshly grated pecorino cheese
	Salt and freshly ground black pepper
½	cup (120 ml) extra-virgin olive oil

1. **To prepare the gnocchi,** cook the carrots and potatoes in a large pan of salted boiling water until tender, 15–20 minutes. Drain well.

2. **Mash** the carrots and potatoes together and let cool a little. Stir in the egg, flour, salt, white pepper, and nutmeg, mixing well with a wooden spoon to obtain a firm dough.

3. **Working** quickly, scoop out pieces of dough and roll them on a lightly floured work surface into long sausage shapes about ¾ inch (2 cm) in diameter. Cut the sausage shapes into pieces about 1 inch (2.5 cm) long. Set the gnocchi out on a floured clean cloth and leave for an hour or two to dry.

4. **If** preferred (this is optional, and slightly tricky, but gives the gnocchi their characteristic shape), press each piece with your thumb onto the tongs of a fork and twist. The gnocchi will have fork marks on one side.

5. **To prepare the arugula sauce,** combine the arugula, garlic, pine nuts, cheese, salt, and pepper in a blender or food processor and process until finely chopped. Transfer to a bowl and gradually stir in the oil.

6. **Cook** the gnocchi in batches in a large pan of salted boiling water until they rise to the surface, 3–4 minutes.

7. **Scoop** them out with a slotted spoon, drain well, and place in a warmed dish. Repeat until all the gnocchi are cooked.

8. **Spoon** the arugula sauce over the gnocchi. Toss gently and serve hot.

baked semolina gnocchi
with parmesan

These delicious gnocchi make a hearty meal. Serve with a green or mixed salad.

- ⊙ Serves 4
- ⊕ 40 minutes
- ⊕ 40 minutes
- 🍴 2

4	cups (1 liter) milk
6	tablespoons (90 g) butter
	Salt and freshly ground white pepper
⅛	teaspoon freshly grated nutmeg
1⅔	cups (250 g) semolina flour
6	tablespoons freshly grated Parmesan cheese
3	large egg yolks, beaten with 1 tablespoon milk
1	cup (125 g) freshly grated Parmesan cheese

1. **Preheat** the oven to 400°F (200°C/gas 6). Butter a large, rectangular baking dish, or four individual baking dishes.

2. **Bring** the milk to a boil with 4 tablespoons of butter, salt, pepper, and nutmeg. Sprinkle in the semolina and beat vigorously with a whisk to prevent clumps from forming.

3. **Simmer** over low heat for 20 minutes, stirring constantly.

4. **Remove** from the heat and let cool. Add 2 tablespoons of the Parmesan and the beaten egg yolks.

5. **Grease** a work surface and pour out the semolina. Smooth it out with a spatula and let cool.

6. **Use** a smooth pastry cutter to cut the dough into 2 ½-inch (6-cm) rounds.

7. **Arrange** the leftover dough scraps in the bottom of the prepared baking dish(es). Top with the dough rounds, overlapping slightly.

8. **Sprinkle** with the remaining 2 tablespoons butter and 4 tablespoons Parmesan.

9. **Bake** for 12–15 minutes, or until golden brown.

10. **Serve** hot.

If you liked this recipe, you will love these as well.

herb gnocchi
168

baked gnocchi with butter & sage
170

carrot & potato gnocchi with arugula sauce
172

grilled
& fried
dishes

grilled summer vegetables

These vegetables make a superb starter or can be served with soft, fresh cheeses and crusty bread for a healthy lunch or snack.

◉ Serves 4	**4**	medium zucchini (courgettes), thinly sliced lengthwise
⬚ 15 minutes	**1**	red bell pepper (capsicum), seeded and cut in strips
✹ 15–20 minutes	**1**	yellow bell pepper (capsicum), seeded and cut in strips
▼ 1		

1	large eggplant (aubergine) with skin, thinly sliced
	Salt and freshly ground black pepper
½	cup (120 ml) extra-virgin olive oil

1. **Prepare** a medium-hot fire in a gas or charcoal grill or preheat an indoor grill pan over high heat.

2. **Brush** all the vegetables lightly with oil before placing them on the grill. Place the zucchini on the grill and cook until tender, 3–4 minutes each side. Place on a serving plate and keep warm.

3. **Place** the bell pepper strips on the grill and cook until tender, about 5 minutes each side. Place on a serving plate and keep warm.

4. **Place** the eggplant slices on the grill and cook until tender, about 5 minutes each side.

5. **Place** the grilled vegetables on a large serving plate. Season with salt and pepper. Drizzle with the oil and serve hot or at room temperature.

If you liked this recipe, you will love these as well.

vegetable skewers
180

vegetable kebabs with mozzarella
182

zucchini with arugula pesto
184

vegetable skewers

These skewers are best prepared over a hot barbecue grill.

⊙ Serves 4	2	zucchini (courgettes)
⬤ 25 minutes	1	eggplant (aubergine)
	1	medium onion
🌡 2 hours	1	small red bell pepper (capsicum)
▦ 20 minutes	1	small yellow bell pepper (capsicum)
	1	small green bell pepper (capsicum)
🍸 1	½	cup (125 ml) extra-virgin olive oil

½ teaspoon hot paprika
Freshly squeezed juice of ½ lemon
1 tablespoon finely chopped fresh herbs (oregano, mint, or thyme) + extra leaves, to garnish
Salt and freshly ground black pepper

1. **Slice** the zucchini into rounds ½ inch (1 cm) thick. Cut the eggplant into slices of the same thickness, and cut into pieces the same size as the zucchini. Cut the bell peppers into 1-inch (2.5-cm) squares.

2. **Thread** the vegetables onto metal skewers. Set in a dish in a single layer. Prepare at least two skewers per person.

3. **Combine** the oil, paprika, lemon juice, and herbs in a small bowl. Season with salt and pepper and whisk well. Pour over the skewers, turning them to coat. Let marinate in the refrigerator for 2 hours.

4. **Prepare** a medium-hot fire in a gas or charcoal barbecue or preheat an indoor grill pan over high heat.

5. **Drain** the skewers, reserving the marinade to baste, and place half on the grill. Cook, turning so that they brown on all sides, until tender, about 10 minutes. Baste with the reserved marinade. Repeat with the remaining skewers.

6. **Serve** hot.

If you liked this recipe, you will love these as well.

grilled summer vegetables

178

vegetable kebabs with mozzarella

182

zucchini with arugula pesto

184

vegetable kebabs
with mozzarella

You could replace the mozzarella in this recipe with the same quantity of halloumi or another local cheese that is good for grilling.

- Serves 4
- 20 minutes
- 15–20 minutes

1

2	zucchini (courgettes), thickly sliced
1	long, slender eggplant (aubergine), thickly sliced
8	baby mozzarella cheeses (bocconcini), cut in half
	About 16 cherry tomatoes

Fresh basil leaves

Salt and freshly ground black pepper

$\frac{1}{2}$ cup (120 ml) extra-virgin olive oil

1. **Prepare** a medium-hot fire in a gas or charcoal barbecue grill, or preheat an indoor grill pan over high heat.

2. **Arrange** the zucchini and eggplant on the grill and cook, turning often, until tender, 7–10 minutes.

3. **Thread** the vegetables onto metal skewers, alternating with the mozzarella, tomatoes, and basil leaves. Season with salt and pepper, and brush with the oil.

4. **Cook** on the grill until the zucchini, eggplant, and tomatoes are beginning to soften and the cheese is starting to melt, about 5 minutes.

5. **Serve** hot.

If you liked this recipe, you will love these as well.

grilled **summer** vegetables

178

vegetable **skewers**

180

zucchini with arugula pesto

184

zucchini with arugula pesto

With only 17 calories in each 3½-ounce (100-g) serving, zucchini are very low in calories. They contain no saturated fats or cholesterol but have plenty of dietary fiber.

- Serves 4
- 25 minutes
- 1 hour
- 30 minutes

- 1

4	zucchini (courgettes), thinly sliced lengthwise
8	tablespoons (125 ml) extra-virgin olive oil
2	tablespoons cider vinegar
1	tablespoon balsamic vinegar
1	clove garlic, thinly sliced
	Salt and freshly ground black pepper
2	cups (100 g) arugula (rocket)
6	tablespoons pine nuts
1–2	tablespoons hot water, optional
4	tablespoons raisins

1. **Place** the zucchini in a small, shallow dish.

2. **Mix** 3 tablespoons of oil, cider vinegar, balsamic vinegar, and garlic in a small bowl. Season with salt and pepper. Pour over the zucchini. Let marinate for 1 hour.

3. **Put** 1½ cups (75 g) of arugula in a blender with 4 tablespoons of pine nuts and the remaining oil and process until smooth. Drain the zucchini, reserving the marinade.

4. **Prepare** a medium-hot fire in a gas or charcoal grill, or preheat an indoor grill pan over high heat.

5. **Cook** the zucchini in batches, turning often until tender, 4–5 minutes each batch.

6. **Arrange** the remaining arugula on a serving platter and place the zucchini on top. Sprinkle the remaining pine nuts and the raisins over the zucchini. Season with salt and pepper, and drizzle with the reserved marinade.

7. **Serve** hot or at room temperature.

If you liked this recipe, you will love these as well.

grilled summer vegetables

178

vegetable skewers

180

vegetable kebabs with mozzarella

182

pan-fried potatoes
with sun-dried tomatoes

Serve these potatoes hot with a frittata (see pages 270–273) and salad.

- Serves 4
- 10 minutes
- 20 minutes

1

1½	pounds (750 g) whole small new potatoes
½	cup (120 ml) extra-virgin olive oil
½	teaspoon sweet paprika
	Salt

6	sun-dried tomatoes packed in oil, drained and finely chopped
1	tablespoon capers, drained
1	teaspoon dried oregano

1. **Bring** a large pot of salted water to a boil, add the potatoes, and cook until almost tender, about 10 minutes (depending on their size).

2. **Drain** well and cut in half.

3. **Heat** the oil in a large frying pan over medium heat. Add the potatoes and sauté for 5 minutes.

4. **Sprinkle** with the paprika and season with salt. Add the sun-dried tomatoes and capers. Sauté until the potatoes are crisp and golden, 3–5 minutes.

5. **Sprinkle** with the oregano and sauté for 1 minute more.

6. **Serve** hot.

If you liked this recipe, you will love these as well.

breaded asparagus with mint dip

188

tomato & basil rice fritters

190

stuffed potato croquettes

192

breaded asparagus
with mint dip

These asparagus make a wonderful appetizer or snack.

 Serves 6

🕐 10 minutes

🍽 20–30 minutes

🍸 1

1	pound (500 g) asparagus, trimmed
2	large eggs
3	tablespoons freshly grated Parmesan cheese
4	cups (1 liter) vegetable oil, for frying

1	cup (150 g) fine, dry bread crumbs
½	cup (120 ml) plain yogurt
½	cup (120 ml) mayonnaise
1	tablespoon finely chopped fresh mint
	Salt

1. **Cook** the asparagus in a large pot of salted boiling water until almost tender, about 5 minutes. Drain well and dry carefully on a clean towel.

2. **Beat** the eggs and Parmesan in a small bowl.

3. **Heat** the oil in a deep-fryer or deep saucepan. Test the oil temperature by dropping in a small piece of bread. If it immediately bubbles to the surface and begins to turn golden, the oil is ready.

4. **Dip** the asparagus in the beaten eggs and then in the bread crumbs, making sure they are well coated.

5. **Fry** the asparagus in small batches until golden brown, 3–4 minutes each batch.

6. **Drain** on paper towels. Beat the yogurt, mayonnaise, and mint in a small bowl.

7. **Season** the asparagus with salt.

8. **Serve** hot straight from the pan, with the mint dip on the side.

If you liked this recipe, you will love these as well.

pan-fried potatoes with sun-dried tomatoes

186

stuffed potato croquettes

192

pumpkin fritters

194

tomato & basil rice fritters

Like most fried dishes, these fritters are best served hot straight from the pan.

- Serves 6
- 30 minutes
- 30 minutes
- 45–50 minutes

- 2

3	tablespoons butter
1	tablespoon extra-virgin olive oil
1	medium onion, finely chopped
2	cloves garlic, finely chopped
2	cups (400 g) Arborio rice
$\frac{1}{2}$	cup (120 ml) dry white wine
1	(14-ounce/400-g) can tomatoes, with juice
1	tablespoon tomato paste (concentrate)
3	cups (750 ml) vegetable stock, boiling

$\frac{1}{3}$	cup (50 g) freshly grated Parmesan cheese
1	cup (50 g) finely chopped fresh basil leaves
	Salt and freshly ground black pepper
4	ounces (120 g) mozzarella cheese, cut into $\frac{3}{4}$-inch (2-cm) cubes
$\frac{1}{2}$	cup (75 g) fine dry bread crumbs
4	cups (1 liter) vegetable oil, for deep frying

1. **Heat** 2 tablespoons of the butter and oil in a large saucepan over medium heat. Add the onion and garlic and cook until softened, 3–4 minutes. Add the rice and cook, stirring to coat, for 2 minutes.

2. **Pour in** the wine, tomatoes, and tomato paste and cook, stirring, until all the liquid has been absorbed. Decrease the heat to medium-low and gradually add the stock $\frac{1}{2}$ cup (125 ml) at a time, stirring until all the liquid is absorbed. Cook, stirring, for 20–25 minutes, or until all the rice is completely tender and cooked through (not al dente, as in traditional risotto).

3. **Stir in** the Parmesan cheese, basil, and the remaining 1 tablespoon butter. Season with salt and pepper.

4. **Spread** the risotto onto a large plate and set aside to cool.

5. **Form** the cooled risotto into walnut-size balls. Place a piece of mozzarella in the center of each and reshape. Coat in bread crumbs, place on a large plate, and refrigerate for 30 minutes, until firm.

6. **Heat** the oil in a deep-fryer or deep saucepan. Test the temperature of the oil by dropping in a small piece of bread. If it immediately bubbles to the surface and begins to turn golden, the oil is ready.

7. **Fry** the fritters in batches in the hot oil until golden brown all over, 5–7 minutes per batch. Scoop out with a slotted spoon and drain on paper towels.

8. **Serve** hot.

stuffed potato croquettes

Make sure that the oil is really hot before you add the croquettes. If it is not hot enough they will absorb a lot of oil during frying, making them heavy and unappetizing.

Serves 6

10 minutes

20 minutes

2

2	pounds (1 kg) potatoes, peeled and cut into small chunks
½	cup (60 g) freshly grated Parmesan cheese
1	tablespoon finely chopped fresh parsley
4	large eggs, lightly beaten Salt and freshly ground black pepper
4	ounces (125 g) mozzarella cheese, cut into cubes
6	sun-dried tomatoes packed in oil, drained and diced
4	cups (1 liter) vegetable oil, for frying
1	cup (150 g) fine, dry bread crumbs

1. **Cook** the potatoes in a large pot of salted, boiling water for 10 minutes, or until tender. Drain and transfer to a large bowl. Mash until smooth.

2. **Mix** in the Parmesan, parsley, and 3 of the eggs. Season with salt and pepper.

3. **Shape** the mixture into 4-inch (10-cm) oblong croquettes.

4. **Press** pieces of mozzarella and sun-dried tomatoes into the center of each croquette.

5. **Heat** the oil in a deep-fryer or deep saucepan. Test the oil temperature by dropping in a small piece of bread. If it immediately bubbles to the surface and begins to turn golden, the oil is ready.

6. **Dip** the croquettes in the remaining beaten egg and then in the bread crumbs.

7. **Fry** until golden brown, turning with tongs in the oil. Scoop out with a slotted spoon and drain on paper towels.

8. **Serve** hot.

If you liked this recipe, you will love these as well.

pan-fried potatoes with sun-dried tomatoes

186

pumpkin fritters

194

corn fritters

196

pumpkin fritters

Choosing the right oil is important when frying food. You should choose an oil that has a high smoking point, such as olive, grapeseed, canola, peanut, safflower, or sunflower oil. These oils are all healthier than a generic "vegetable oil" when it comes to frying.

Serves 6

20 minutes

30–35 minutes

2

2	cups (300 g) pumpkin or winter squash flesh, cut into 1-inch (2.5-cm) cubes
3	large eggs, 1 left whole and 2 separated
1	cup (150 g) all-purpose (plain) flour
½	cup (75 g) crumbled amaretto cookies or graham cracker crumbs
2	tablespoons freshly grated Parmesan cheese
½	teaspoon baking powder
¼	teaspoon freshly grated nutmeg
½	teaspoon salt
4	cups (1 liter) vegetable oil, for deep frying

1. **Bring** a large pot of salted water to a boil. Add the pumpkin and cook until tender, about 5 minutes,

2. **Drain** and process in a food processor until puréed. Transfer to a large bowl and mix in the whole egg and 2 egg yolks, the flour, amaretto cookies, Parmesan, baking powder, nutmeg, and salt.

3. **Beat** the egg whites until stiff. Gently fold the whites into the pumpkin mixture. Heat the oil in a deep-fryer or deep saucepan. Test the oil

temperature by dropping in a small piece of bread. If it immediately bubbles to the surface and begins to turn golden, the oil is ready.

4. **Fry** tablespoons of the mixture in small batches, turning once or twice with tongs until golden brown and crisp, 5–7 minutes.

5. **Remove** with a slotted spoon and drain well on paper towels.

6. **Serve** hot.

If you liked this recipe, you will love these as well.

tomato & basil fritters

190

stuffed potato croquettes

192

corn fritters

196

corn fritters

These fritters are deliciously sweet.

- Serves 4
- 20 minutes
- 20–30 minutes

2

²⁄₃	cup (100 g) all-purpose (plain) flour
2	large eggs, lightly beaten
²⁄₃	cup (150 ml) milk
1	(14-ounce/400-g) can corn (sweet corn), drained
³⁄₄	cup (90 g) freshly grated Parmesan cheese
	Freshly ground black pepper
4	cups (1 liter) vegetable oil, for deep frying

1. **Mix** the flour, eggs, milk, corn, and Parmesan in a large bowl until well blended. Season with pepper.

2. **Heat** the oil in a deep-fryer or deep saucepan.

3. **Test** the oil temperature by dropping in a small piece of bread. If it immediately bubbles to the surface and begins to turn golden, the oil is ready.

4. **Fry** tablespoons of the corn mixture in small batches, turning with tongs until golden brown, 5–7 minutes.

5. **Remove** with a slotted spoon and drain well on paper towels.

6. **Serve** hot.

If you liked this recipe, you will love these as well.

pumpkin fritters

194

spicy peanut fritters

198

vegetable samosas

202

spicy peanut fritters

Serve these peanut fritters with plenty of sweet chili sauce for dipping.

- Serves 6
- 30 minutes
- 15–20 minutes

- 2

1¼	cups (200 g) raw peanuts
1	teaspoon coriander seeds
2	teaspoons finely chopped fresh ginger
2	cloves garlic
1	teaspoon crushed red pepper flakes, or 2 small dried chiles, crumbled
1	teaspoon salt

½	teaspoon ground turmeric
1	cup (150 g) rice flour
⅔	cup (100 g) all-purpose (plain) flour
1	cup (250 ml) coconut milk
4	cups (1 liter) vegetable oil, for deep frying
½	cup (120 ml) Thai sweet chili sauce, to serve

1. **Put** the peanuts in a wok and dry-fry over low heat for 5 minutes. Rub to remove the skins and coarsely chop.

2. **Combine** the coriander seeds, ginger, garlic, red pepper flakes, salt, and turmeric in a food processor and process until finely chopped.

3. **Sift** both flours into a large bowl. Stir in the spice mixture and coconut milk, blending well. Add the peanuts.

4. **Heat** the oil in a deep-fryer or deep saucepan. Test the oil temperature by dropping in a small piece of bread.

5. **If** it immediately bubbles to the surface and begins to turn golden, the oil is ready.

6. **Add** tablespoons of the batter in small batches. Fry, turning with tongs until golden brown, 3–5 minutes.

7. **Remove** with a slotted spoon and drain well on paper towels. Serve hot with the chili sauce.

If you liked this recipe, you will love these as well.

stuffed potato croquettes

192

pumpkin fritters

194

corn fritters

196

tomato croquettes

These croquettes take some skill to prepare but once you get them right they really are a special treat. Serve hot, with a large mixed salad.

- ⬤ Serves 4–6
- 🕒 20 minutes
- 🕒 30 minutes

- 🍴 3

1	pound (500 g) ripe tomatoes
12	ounces (350 g) ricotta cheese, drained
2	large egg yolks + 2 large eggs, beaten until foamy
2	tablespoons finely chopped fresh parsley
¼	teaspoon freshly grated nutmeg

Salt and freshly ground black pepper

1	cup (150 g) fine dry bread crumbs + 1–2 tablespoons as needed
1	cup (150 g) all-purpose (plain) flour
4	cups (1 liter) vegetable oil, for deep frying

1. **Blanch** the tomatoes in boiling water for 1 minute.

2. **Drain** and peel. Remove the seeds, chop coarsely, and let drain.

3. **Mix** the ricotta and egg yolks in a large bowl until smooth. Add the tomatoes, parsley, and nutmeg. Season with salt and pepper and mix well. The mixture should be firm; if it is too runny, add 1–2 tablespoons of dry bread crumbs.

4. **Form** into oblong croquettes about 2 inches (4-cm) long and 1 inch (2.5-cm) thick. Roll in the flour, dip in the beaten egg, then roll in the bread crumbs.

5. **Heat** the oil in a deep-fryer or deep saucepan. Test the oil temperature by dropping in a small piece of bread. If it immediately bubbles to the surface and begins to turn golden, the oil is ready.

6. **Fry** the croquettes in small batches, turning with tongs until golden brown, 5–7 minutes.

7. **Remove** with a slotted spoon and drain on paper towels.

8. **Serve** hot.

If you liked this recipe, you will love these as well.

pan-fried potatoes with sun-dried tomatoes

186

tomato & basil rice fritters

190

stuffed potato croquettes

192

vegetable samosas

Samosas are a traditional Indian appetizer.

Serves 6

30 minutes

30 minutes

45 minutes

3

SAMOSA PASTRY

2	cups (300 g) all-purpose (plain) flour
1	teaspoon salt
2	tablespoons (60 ml) vegetable oil
7	tablespoons warm water

FILLING

8	ounces (250 g) potatoes, peeled
2	tablespoons Asian sesame oil
1	teaspoon brown mustard seeds
1	onion, finely diced
2	garlic cloves, minced
3	curry leaves (optional)
1/2	teaspoon garam masala
1/2	teaspoon ground turmeric
1/2	teaspoon ground coriander
1/2	teaspoon ground cumin
1/4	teaspoon ground chile
1	cup (150 g) frozen peas
1	tablespoon freshly squeezed lemon juice
	Vegetable oil, for frying
1	cup (250 ml) yogurt mixed with 2 tablespoons finely chopped fresh mint, to serve

1. **To prepare the pastry,** sift the flour and salt into a medium bowl. Add the 2 tablespoons of oil and gradually add the water, kneading until a dough forms. Knead on a floured work surface until smooth and elastic, about 10 minutes. Shape into a ball and transfer to a lightly oiled bowl. Cover and let rest for 30 minutes.

2. **To prepare the filling,** cook the potatoes in a pot of salted boiling water until tender. Drain and set aside to cool slightly.

3. **Heat** the 2 tablespoons of oil in a saucepan over medium-low heat. Add the mustard seeds, onion, garlic, curry leaves, garam masala, turmeric, coriander, cumin, and ground chile and sauté until the onion is soft and the spices are fragrant, 3–4 minutes.

4. **Dice** the potatoes and add to the pan. Add the peas and lemon juice and stir to combine. Remove from the heat and set aside to cool.

5. **Knead** the pastry for 2–3 minutes, then divide into eight balls. Roll out one of the balls on a lightly floured work surface into a 7-inch (18 cm) disk. Cut the disk in half, moisten the edge with a little water, and form into a cone in your hand. Fill the cone three-quarters full with the filling. Moisten the inside edge of the opening and seal, pressing the edge with the prongs of a fork. Repeat the process with the remaining dough and filling.

6. **Pour** about 2 inches (5 cm) of oil into a wok. Test the oil temperature by dropping in a small piece of bread. If it immediately bubbles to the surface and begins to turn golden, the oil is ready.

7. **Fry** the samosas in batches, turning often with tongs until golden brown and crisp, 3–5 minutes. Remove with a slotted spoon and drain on paper towels.

8. **Serve** hot, with the minted yogurt.

stir-fries,
stews
& curries

stir-fried vegetables
with noodles

Stir-fried vegetables are crunchy, brightly colored, and full of flavor and goodness.

Serves 4

15 minutes

5–10 minutes

1

12	ounces (350 g) dried Chinese egg noodles
2	tablespoons Asian sesame oil
4	scallions (spring onions), coarsely chopped
2	teaspoons finely chopped fresh ginger
2	cloves garlic, finely chopped
2	cups (300 g) frozen peas

32	cherry tomatoes, halved
2	tablespoons finely chopped fresh parsley
2	tablespoons finely chopped fresh basil
2	tablespoons finely chopped fresh cilantro (coriander)
2	tablespoons finely chopped fresh chives
2	tablespoons light soy sauce

1. **Cook** the noodles according to the instructions on the package. Drain well.

2. **Heat** the oil in a large wok over medium-high heat. Add the scallions, ginger, garlic, and peas and stir-fry for 2–3 minutes.

3. **Add** the tomatoes, herbs, soy sauce, and noodles and stir-fry for 2 more minutes.

4. **Serve** hot.

If you liked this recipe, you will love these as well.

pad thai 208

spicy vegetarian stew 210

potato, green bean & tomato stew 214

pad thai

Pad Thai is a dried rice noodle dish from Thailand. There are many variations; ours is a delicious vegetarian version.

Serves 4

15 minutes

10 minutes

1

- 14 ounces (400 g) dried Thai rice noodles
- 2 tablespoons peanut oil
- 2 cloves garlic, sliced
- 1/4 Chinese cabbage (wom bok), chopped
- 8 ounces (250 g) firm tofu, cubed
- 4 large eggs, beaten
- 3 tablespoons finely grated jaggery (palm sugar) or brown sugar
- 1 1/2 tablespoons tamarind paste
- 1 1/2 tablespoons light soy sauce
- 1 1/2 tablespoons Thai sweet chili sauce
- 3 cups (150 g) mung bean sprouts
- 5 scallions (spring onions), cut into 2-inch (5-cm) lengths
- 1/2 cup fresh cilantro (coriander) leaves
- 1/4 cup (40 g) roasted peanuts, chopped
- 1 lime, quartered

1. **Put** the noodles in a medium bowl, add boiling water to cover, and soak for 5 minutes, or until softened. Drain and set aside.

2. **Heat** the oil in a large wok over medium-high heat. Add the garlic and cook until softened, about 30 seconds.

3. **Add** the Chinese cabbage and tofu and stir-fry for 1 minute, or until the cabbage begins to soften. Push to the side, add the eggs, and cook, stirring to scramble for 1 minute.

4. **Decrease** the heat to medium. Add the noodles, jaggery, tamarind paste, soy sauce, and chili sauce and stir-fry for 1 minute. Add the bean sprouts and scallions and stir-fry for another 1 minute, tossing to combine.

5. **Divide** the pad Thai among 4–6 serving plates and top with cilantro and peanuts.

6. **Serve** hot, with lime wedges to garnish.

If you liked this recipe, you will love these as well.

stir-fried vegetables with noodles

206

caponata with rice

212

bell pepper & potato stew

216

spicy vegetarian stew

Vary the vegetables in this stew according to what you like or have in the refrigerator.

Serves 4

30 minutes

40 minutes

1

2	tablespoons peanut oil
1	teaspoon cumin seeds
1	onion, thinly sliced
2	stalks celery, chopped
2	cloves garlic, sliced
1	teaspoon green curry paste
1	red bell pepper (capsicum), seeded and sliced
2	zucchini (courgettes), sliced
1	medium eggplant (aubergine), chopped
8	ounces (250 g) button mushrooms, quartered

2	(14-ounce/400-g) cans tomatoes, with juice
1	tablespoon Thai sweet chili sauce
1	teaspoon chili powder
2	teaspoons ground coriander
1	(14-ounce/400-g) can red kidney beans
	Freshly squeezed juice of 1 lemon
	Cilantro (coriander)
	Freshly cooked basmati rice, to serve

1. **Heat** the oil in a large saucepan over medium heat. Add the cumin seeds and sauté until fragrant, about 2 minutes.

2. **Add** the onion, celery, garlic, and curry paste and cook until the onions are softened, about 5 minutes.

3. **Add** the bell pepper, zucchini, eggplant, mushrooms, and tomatoes. Cover and simmer over medium heat until the vegetables begin to soften, about 5 minutes.

4. **Add** the chili sauce, chili powder, ground cumin, and coriander. Mix well, then add the kidney beans. Cover and cook until the vegetables are tender, about 25 minutes, stirring occasionally.

5. **Stir** in the lemon juice and cilantro. Serve hot over the rice.

If you liked this recipe, you will love these as well.

pad thai

208

red bean chili

224

vegetarian curry with brown rice

228

caponata with rice

Caponata is a traditional vegetable dish from Sicily. The sweetness of the pear contrasts beautifully with the salty olives and the vegetables. It is always served with rice.

Serves 4

20 minutes

40–45 minutes

1

5	tablespoons extra-virgin olive oil
2	eggplants (aubergines), diced
1	small onion, coarsely chopped
2	stalks celery, finely chopped
4	large tomatoes, coarsely chopped
1	firm-ripe pear, peeled and coarsely chopped
1	cup (100 g) black olives

1	tablespoon salt-cured capers, rinsed
1	tablespoon sugar
	Salt and freshly ground black pepper
¼	cup (60 ml) water
2	tablespoons red wine vinegar
1½	cups (300 g) short-grain rice
1	tablespoon finely chopped fresh basil

1. **Heat** 3 tablespoons of the oil in a large frying pan over medium heat. Add the eggplants and onion and sauté until softened, about 10 minutes.

2. **Add** the celery, tomatoes, pear, olives, capers, and sugar. Season with salt and pepper. Add the water and vinegar. Simmer over low heat for about 15 minutes, or until all the vegetables have softened.

3. **Meanwhile**, bring a large pot of salted water to a boil. Add the rice and cook until tender, 12–15 minutes.

4. **Drain** and drizzle with the remaining 2 tablespoons of oil. Stir in the basil.

5. **Oil** four small ¾-cup (180-ml) molds with oil and fill with the seasoned rice, pressing down firmly with the back of a spoon.

6. **Turn** the rice out of the molds onto a serving dish and serve with the caponata.

If you liked this recipe, you will love these as well.

bell pepper & potato stew

216

vegetarian curry with brown rice

228

pineapple curry with coconut

230

potato, green bean & tomato stew

You can vary this stew by replacing the potatoes with sweet potatoes.

- Serves 4
- 20 minutes
- 40–50 minutes

- 2

12	ounces (350 g) potatoes, peeled and coarsely chopped
12	ounces (350 g) green beans, topped and tailed
¼	cup (60 ml) extra-virgin olive oil
1	onion, finely chopped
1	clove garlic, finely chopped
1	tablespoon finely chopped fresh parsley
	Salt and freshly ground black pepper
3	large tomatoes, peeled and coarsely chopped

1. **Bring** a pot of salted water to a boil. Add the potatoes and cook until almost tender, 15–20 minutes. Drain and set aside.

2. **Blanch** the green beans in salted boiling water until almost tender, 5 minutes. Drain and chop into short lengths.

3. **Heat** the oil in a large frying pan over medium heat. Add the onion, garlic, and parsley and sauté until the garlic is pale gold, 3–4 minutes. Season with salt and pepper. Add the tomatoes and simmer for 10 minutes.

4. **Stir** in the potatoes and green beans and simmer until tender, 10–15 more minutes.

5. **Serve** hot.

If you liked this recipe, you will love these as well.

spicy vegetarian stew

210

bell pepper & potato stew

216

mushroom stew with pine nuts

218

bell pepper & potato stew

This hearty stew makes a delicious weeknight supper.

Serves 4

10 minutes

35–40 minutes

1

- ¼ cup (60 ml) extra-virgin olive oil
- 2 medium potatoes, peeled and cut into small cubes
- 1 large onion, finely chopped
- 1 red bell pepper (capsicum), seeded and cut into small chunks
- 1 green bell pepper (capsicum), seeded and cut into small chunks
- 1 eggplant (aubergine), cut into small cubes
- 1 large zucchini (courgette), cut into small cubes
- 4 large tomatoes, coarsely chopped
  Salt and freshly ground black pepper
- ¼ cup (60 ml) water, optional
- 1 tablespoon finely chopped basil or parsley, to serve

1. **Heat** the oil in a large frying pan or flameproof casserole over medium heat. Add the potatoes and sauté until golden, 8–10 minutes.

2. **Add** the onion and bell peppers and sauté until the onion is lightly browned, 8–10 minutes.

3. **Add** the eggplant and zucchini and cook for 5 minutes.

4. **Stir** in the tomatoes. Season with salt and pepper. Simmer until the vegetables are tender, 10–15 minutes, adding the water if the mixture begins to stick to the pan.

5. **Serve** hot, sprinkled with the basil or parsley.

If you liked this recipe, you will love these as well.

spicy vegetarian stew

210

potato, green bean & tomato stew

214

green bean & zucchini ratatouille

220

mushroom stew
with pine nuts

The pine nuts add delicious flavor and protein to this stew.

 Serves 4

10 minutes

20 minutes

1

$\frac{1}{4}$	cup (60 ml) extra-virgin olive oil
2	large potatoes, diced
2	cloves garlic, finely chopped
$1\frac{1}{2}$	pounds (750 g) fresh white mushrooms, trimmed and coarsely chopped

	Salt and freshly ground black pepper
$\frac{2}{3}$	cup (120 g) pine nuts
$\frac{1}{2}$	cup (50 g) slivered almonds
1	tablespoon coarsely chopped fresh mint

1. **Heat** the oil in a large frying pan over medium heat. Add the potatoes and garlic and sauté until the garlic is pale gold, 3–4 minutes.

2. **Add** the mushrooms and season with salt and pepper. Cover and cook for 5 minutes.

3. **Uncover** and let the moisture evaporate. Stir in the pine nuts and almonds and cook for 10 minutes.

4. **Sprinkle** with the mint just before removing from heat.

5. **Serve** hot.

If you liked this recipe, you will love these as well.

spicy vegetarian stew

210

bell pepper & potato stew

216

pumpkin & lentil tagine

222

green bean & zucchini ratatouille

This is a variation on the classic French ratatouille.

Serves 4

15 minutes

40–45 minutes

1

$\frac{1}{3}$ cup (90 ml) extra-virgin olive oil + extra to drizzle

5 cloves garlic, 2 unpeeled and whole, 3 peeled and sliced

3 zucchini (courgettes), halved lengthwise, and cut into 1-inch (2.5-cm) pieces

1 large red bell pepper (capsicum), seeded and cut into $\frac{1}{2}$-inch (1-cm) strips

1 red onion, thinly sliced

1 white onion, thinly sliced

1 tablespoon coriander seeds, coarsely crushed

1 pound (500 g) cherry tomatoes, halved

2 tablespoons thyme leaves, or 1 teaspoon dried thyme

3 tablespoons finely chopped fresh parsley
Salt

8 ounces (250 g) green beans, trimmed and halved widthwise

8 ounces (250 g) sugar snaps or snow peas (mangetout), trimmed and sliced

5 ounces (150 g) shelled baby fava (broad) beans
Water, optional
Freshly squeezed juice of 1 lemon
Freshly ground black pepper

1. **Heat** half the oil in a large frying pan or wide saucepan over medium heat. Add the whole garlic cloves and sauté for 1 minute. Add the zucchini and sauté until lightly browned, about 5 minutes. Lift out with a spatula and place on paper towels to drain.

2. **Sauté** the bell pepper in the same oil until slightly browned, 3–5 minutes. Lift out the pepper and garlic and set aside with the zucchini.

3. **Reduce** the heat, add the remaining oil, and add both onions. Sauté over low heat until soft but not browned, 8–10 minutes. Add the sliced garlic and coriander, and sauté for 1 minute.

4. **Add** the tomatoes, thyme, and 2 tablespoons of the parsley. Season with a good pinch of salt. Cover and cook until the tomatoes are soft, about 10 minutes.

5. **Add** the green beans and simmer, covered, for 4 minutes. Add the sugar snaps and fava beans, and mix in well.

6. **Return** the zucchini and peppers to the frying pan. Slip the peel off the fried garlic clove, mash, and stir into the mixture. Bring the vegetables back to the simmering point.

7. **Simmer**, uncovered, until all the vegetables are soft and the ratatouille is thick, 8–10 minutes. Stir frequently, adding a few tablespoons of water if the ratatouille is sticking to the bottom.

8. **Taste** and season with salt, pepper, and lemon juice.

9. **Sprinkle** with the remaining 1–2 tablespoons parsley and drizzle with olive oil.

10. **Serve** warm or at room temperature.

pumpkin & lentil tagine

This is a hearty dish that can easily be served as a one-pot meal.

Serves 4–6

30 minutes

30–40 minutes

1

2	cups (200 g) Le Puy lentils
8	cups (2 liters) water
2	medium tomatoes
3	tablespoons extra-virgin olive oil
1	large onion, diced
4	garlic cloves, finely chopped
1½	teaspoons sweet paprika
1	teaspoon turmeric
1	teaspoon ground cumin
½	teaspoon ground cayenne pepper
1	tablespoon tomato paste
½	teaspoon sugar
1½	pounds (750 g) winter squash or pumpkin, peeled and cubed
3	tablespoons finely chopped fresh parsley
4	tablespoons chopped cilantro (coriander)
	Salt and freshly ground black pepper

1. **Put** the lentils and water in a medium saucepan over high heat and bring to a boil. Decrease the heat to low, cover, and cook until just tender, 20–30 minutes.

2. **Cut** the tomatoes in half crosswise and squeeze out the seeds. Coarsely grate the flesh into a small bowl and discard the skins.

3. **Heat** the oil in a large saucepan over medium heat. Add the onion and garlic and cook until softened, 3–4 minutes.

4. **Add** the paprika, turmeric, cumin, and cayenne and cook until fragrant, 30 seconds. Add the tomato, tomato paste, and sugar and stir to combine. Add the squash and lentils with their cooking liquid and bring to a boil. Decrease the heat to low, cover, and cook until the squash is tender, 15–20 minutes.

5. **Stir in** the parsley and cilantro and season with salt and pepper. Serve hot.

If you liked this recipe, you will love these as well.

mushroom stew with pine nuts

218

red bean chili

224

spicy potato curry

226

red bean chili

Another filling dish that can be served as a tasty one-dish meal.

Serves 4

30 minutes

30–40 minutes

1

½	cup bulgur wheat
1¼	cups (300 ml) water, boiling
2	tablespoons vegetable oil
1	large onion, diced
1	stalk celery, diced
2	garlic cloves, sliced
2	large red bell peppers (capsicums), seeded and diced
1	teaspoon ground cumin
1	teaspoon cayenne pepper
1	(14-ounce/400-g) can kidney beans, drained

1	(14-ounce/400-g) can tomatoes, with juice
2	tablespoons tomato paste (concentrate)
1	red chili, chopped
1	tablespoon red wine vinegar
2	teaspoons sugar
	Salt and freshly ground black pepper
	Jasmine rice, to serve
¾	cup (180 g) sour cream, to serve
	Fresh parsley

1. **Put** the bulgur wheat in a small bowl, pour in 1 cup (250 ml) of the boiling water, cover, and set aside.

2. **Heat** the oil in a medium saucepan over medium-low heat. Add the onion, celery, and garlic and sauté until softened, about 5 minutes.

3. **Add** the bell peppers, cumin, and cayenne and cook for 1 minute, or until fragrant. Add the kidney beans, tomatoes, tomato paste, chili, vinegar, and sugar. Stir in the bulgur and the remaining ¼ cup (60 ml) water and bring to a boil. Decrease the heat to low and cook until the stew has thickened and the flavors have developed, 15–20 minutes. Season with salt and pepper.

4. **Serve** hot with the rice and topped with sour cream and parsley.

If you liked this recipe, you will love these as well.

mushroom stew with pine nuts

218

pumpkin & lentil tagine

222

vegetarian curry with brown rice

228

spicy potato curry

If using baby or new potatoes in this curry, leave the peel on.

🔘 Serves 4

🕐 20 minutes

🍳 35–40 minutes

🍴 2

2 pounds (1 kg) potatoes, peeled and cubed
2 scallions (spring onions), white and green parts separated, finely chopped
2 cloves garlic, finely chopped
1 fresh green chili, seeded and finely chopped
1 teaspoon salt
1 (2/3-inch/1.5-cm) piece fresh ginger, peeled and sliced

Seeds from 2 cardamom pods
2 tablespoons peanut oil
1 tablespoon butter
1 stick cinnamon
2 large tomatoes, chopped
1 teaspoon mustard seeds
1 tablespoon garam masala
1/2 cup (120 ml) plain yogurt
Fresh cilantro (coriander), to garnish

1. **Bring** a large pot of salted water to a boil. Add the potatoes and cook until almost tender, 15 minutes. Drain well.

2. **Combine** the white part of the scallions with the garlic, chile, salt, ginger, and cardamom seeds in a food processor and process to make a paste.

3. **Heat** the oil and butter in a large frying pan over low heat. Add the spice paste and sauté for 2 minutes.

4. **Add** the cinnamon, tomatoes, mustard seeds, and garam masala and simmer for 5 minutes, stirring constantly.

5. **Stir** in the yogurt and cook until the sauce has thickened slightly, 2 minutes.

6. **Add** the potatoes and cook until tender, 5–10 minutes.

7. **Transfer** to a serving dish. Garnish with the green part of the scallions and cilantro. **Serve hot.**

If you liked this recipe, you will love these as well.

bell pepper & potato stew

216

pumpkin & lentil tagine

222

vegetarian curry with brown rice

228

vegetarian curry with brown rice

The coconut milk will tone down the heat of the curry. If you like spicy food, garnish the curry with a thinly sliced red or green chili or dust with 1 teaspoon of red pepper flakes.

Serves 4

15 minutes

45 minutes

1

1	cup (150 g) winter squash or pumpkin
2	tablespoons peanut oil
½	teaspoon mustard seeds
½	teaspoon cumin seeds
2	green chilies, sliced
2	cloves garlic, sliced
1	teaspoon minced ginger
2	onions, finely chopped
4	zucchini (courgettes) sliced
2	large potatoes, peeled and cubed
4	ounces (125 g) okra, sliced

4	ounces (120 g) button mushrooms, halved
½	teaspoon white pepper
1	tablespoon Worcestershire sauce
2	tablespoons soy sauce
2	cups (500 ml) vegetable stock
½	cup (120 ml) coconut milk
	Fresh cilantro (coriander), to garnish
	Freshly cooked brown rice, to serve

1. **Peel** and cube the squash.

2. **Heat** the oil in a large saucepan over medium heat. Add the mustard and cumin seeds and stir until fragrant, 2–3 minutes.

3. **Add** the chilies, garlic, ginger, and onions and sauté until softened, about 5 minutes.

4. **Stir** in the zucchini, potatoes, okra, winter squash, and mushrooms. Add the white pepper, Worcestershire sauce, and soy sauce. Pour in the stock, cover, and simmer until the vegetables are tender and the liquid is reduced a little, about 30 minutes.

5. **Stir** in the cream and simmer for 5 minutes more.

6. **Garnish** with the cilantro and serve hot over the brown rice.

If you liked this recipe, you will love these as well.

mushroom stew with pine nuts

218

spicy potato curry

226

pineapple curry with coconut

228

pineapple curry with coconut

Serve this exotic dish with freshly cooked basmati rice.

⊙ Serves 4

🕐 25 minutes

🕐 20 minutes

🍸 1

SPICE PASTE

6	dried red chilies
1	teaspoon coriander seeds
2	cloves garlic
6	shallots, chopped
1	teaspoon turmeric
1	tablespoon fresh ginger

CURRY

3	tablespoons peanut oil
3	cups (750 ml) coconut milk
1	pineapple, cubed
2	star anise

1	stick cinnamon
1/4	teaspoon ground cloves
1/4	teaspoon ground nutmeg
1	stalk lemongrass, finely chopped
1	tablespoon freshly squeezed lime juice
	Salt and freshly ground black pepper
2	shallots, sliced
	Freshly cooked basmati rice, to serve

1. **To prepare the spice paste,** grind the chilies, coriander seeds, garlic, shallots, turmeric, and ginger in a pestle and mortar.

2. **To prepare the curry,** heat 2 tablespoons of the oil in a large wok or frying pan over medium-high heat. Add the spice paste and sauté until aromatic, 1–2 minutes.

3. **Pour** in the coconut milk and bring to a boil.

4. **Add** the pineapple, star anise, cinnamon, cloves, nutmeg, lemongrass, and lime juice. Season with salt and pepper. Cook over medium heat until the pineapple is heated through, 5–7 minutes.

5. **Heat** the remaining 1 tablespoon of oil in a small frying pan over medium heat. Add the shallots and fry until golden brown, about 5 minutes.

6. **Garnish** the curry with the fried shallots and serve hot with the rice.

If you liked this recipe, you will love these as well.

pumpkin & lentil tagine

222

spicy potato curry

226

vegetarian curry with brown rice

228

casseroles & gratins

provençal bake

Serve this tasty mixed vegetable bake for lunch with plenty of freshly baked bread.

Serves 4

30 minutes

1½–2 hours

1

10	scallions (spring onions), thinly sliced
5	large ripe tomatoes, peeled and chopped
1	medium eggplant (aubergine), chopped into cubes
2	zucchini (courgettes), cut into rounds
1	red bell pepper (capsicum), seeded and coarsely chopped
1	yellow bell pepper (capsicum), seeded and coarsely chopped
1	green bell pepper (capsicum), seeded and coarsely chopped
6	cloves garlic, peeled and finely chopped
⅓	cup (90 ml) extra-virgin olive oil + extra if needed
1	teaspoon salt
1	sprig rosemary
1	bay leaf
1	lemon, halved and quartered

1. **Preheat** the oven to 350°F (180°C/gas 4).

2. **Combine** the scallions, tomatoes, eggplant, zucchini, bell peppers, and garlic in a bowl. Stir in the oil and salt.

3. **Mix** well, then transfer to a large baking dish.

4. **Add** the rosemary and bay leaf, and arrange the lemon quarters on top. Cover with aluminum foil and bake for 1½–2 hours, stirring every 20 minutes and adding more oil if the vegetables dry out.

5. **Serve** hot or at room temperature.

If you liked this recipe, you will love these as well.

bubbling brussels sprouts

236

tomato & zucchini gratin

240

zucchini lasagna
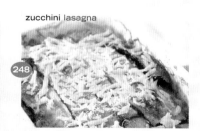
248

bubbling brussels sprouts

An excellent source of vitamins K and C and a very good source of dietary fiber, omega-3 fatty acids, and many other vitamins and minerals, Brussels sprouts are always a healthy food choice.

Serves 4

15 minutes

20–25 minutes

1

- 1 1/2 pounds (750 g) Brussels sprouts
- 5 ounces (150 g) blue cheese, crumbled
- 2 ounces (60 g) chèvre or other fresh goat cheese
- 1 tablespoon coarse-grain mustard
- 1 tablespoon finely chopped fresh parsley
- 1 1/4 cups (300 ml) heavy (double) cream or reduced-fat crème fraîche
- 1/4 cup (60 ml) milk
  Salt and freshly ground black pepper
  Nutmeg
- 2 tablespoons freshly grated Parmesan cheese

1. **Preheat** the oven to 375°F (190°C/ gas 5). Lightly butter a medium baking dish.

2. **Remove** any unsightly outer leaves from the sprouts, trim the bottom of each one, and cut in half.

3. **Bring** a large pot of salted water to a boil. Add the sprouts and return to a boil. Cook for 3 minutes.

4. **Drain** the sprouts and transfer to the prepared baking dish. Sprinkle with the blue cheese and dot with teaspoons of the goat cheese.

5. **Put** the mustard and parsley in a small bowl and whisk in the cream and milk. Season with a salt and pepper and a grating of nutmeg. Pour over the sprouts. Sprinkle the Parmesan on top.

6. **Bake** for 15–20 minutes, until a golden crust has formed and the creamy sauce is bubbling.

7. **Serve** hot.

If you liked this recipe, you will love these as well.

provençal bake

234

tomato & zucchini gratin

240

eggplant bake

246

bell peppers
with mushroom couscous

Bell peppers are low in calories and loaded with good nutrition. They are excellent sources of vitamins A and C, potassium, folic acid, and fiber.

Serves 4

15 minutes

40–45 minutes

1

3	large red bell peppers (capsicums), halved and seeds and core removed
1	cup (150 g) couscous
1/4	cup (60 ml) extra-virgin olive oil
8	ounces (250 g) button mushrooms, trimmed and coarsely chopped
1	clove garlic, finely chopped
10	cherry tomatoes
6	scallions (spring onions), finely chopped
1	tablespoon finely chopped fresh mint
2	tablespoons finely chopped fresh cilantro (coriander) + extra, to garnish
	Freshly squeezed juice of 1/2 lemon
	Salt and freshly ground black pepper
3/4	cup (180 ml) plain yogurt

1. **Preheat** the oven to 400°F (200°C/gas 6).

2. **Prepare** the couscous according to the instructions on the package.

3. **Heat** the oil in a large frying pan over medium heat. Add the mushrooms and sauté for 3 minutes.

4. **Add** the garlic, tomatoes, scallions, mint, and cilantro. Simmer over low heat for 5 minutes.

5. **Add** the couscous and cook for 3 minutes. Drizzle with the lemon juice and season with salt and pepper.

6. **Spoon** the mixture into the bell peppers. Place in a large, oiled baking dish. Cover with aluminum foil and bake for about 45 minutes, until the bell peppers are tender.

7. **Garnish** with the cilantro and serve hot with a dollop or two of yogurt on each one.

If you liked this recipe, you will love these as well.

stuffed vegetables

242

roasted vegetables with rice

250

stuffed eggplant

256

tomato & zucchini gratin

Serve this tasty gratin with a platter of fresh cheeses.

- Serves 4
- 15 minutes
- 25–30 minutes

- 1

6 slices white or whole-wheat (wholemeal) bread, crusts removed

⅓ cup (90 ml) extra-virgin olive oil

2 tablespoons finely chopped fresh cilantro (coriander)

1 tablespoon finely chopped fresh thyme

Salt and freshly ground black pepper

1 pound (500 g) tomatoes, thinly sliced

1 pound (500 g) zucchini (courgettes), very thinly sliced lengthwise

1. **Preheat** the oven to 400°F (200°C/ gas 6).

2. **Put** the bread in the bowl of a food processor and process for 30 seconds to make bread crumbs.

3. **Add** 2 tablespoons of oil, the cilantro, and thyme. Season with salt and pepper. Blend until well mixed.

4. **Layer** the tomatoes and zucchini in a large baking dish. Sprinkle with the bread crumb mixture and drizzle with the remaining oil.

5. **Bake** for about 25–30 minutes, until lightly browned on top.

6. **Serve** hot.

If you liked this recipe, you will love these as well.

bubbling brussels sprouts
236

savory bake
244

zucchini lasagna
248

stuffed vegetables

These vegetables make a hearty main course.

- Serves 6
- 20 minutes
- 30–40 minutes

2

6	large ripe tomatoes	$\frac{1}{2}$	cup (120 ml) extra-virgin olive oil
6	small bell peppers (capsicums), mixed colors	2	tablespoons balsamic vinegar
6	zucchini (courgettes)		Salt and freshly ground black pepper
6	white onions, peeled		
3	long thin eggplant (aubergines)	2	tablespoons finely chopped fresh parsley

1. **Preheat** the oven to 450°F (225°C/gas 7). Lightly oil a large baking pan.

2. **Heat** a little water in the bottom of a steamer.

3. **Cut** the tomatoes, bell peppers, zucchini, onions, and eggplant in half horizontally.

4. **Remove** the seeds from the bell peppers and scoop or cut out the flesh from one half of each of the onions, zucchini, tomatoes, and eggplant. Chop the scooped-out flesh with the remaining halves of the vegetables.

5. **Steam** the hollowed-out vegetables for 5 minutes.

6. **Heat** $\frac{1}{4}$ cup (60 ml) of oil in a large frying pan over high heat. Add the chopped vegetables and sauté until softened, 5–6 minutes.

7. **Add** the vinegar and season with salt, pepper, and parsley.

8. **Place** the steamed vegetable halves in the prepared baking dish. Fill with the cooked filling. Drizzle with the remaining $\frac{1}{4}$ cup (60 ml) oil.

9. **Bake** for 20–30 minutes, until the vegetables are tender.

10. **Serve** hot.

If you liked this recipe, you will love these as well.

bell peppers with mushroom couscous
238

roasted vegetables with rice
250

stuffed eggplant
256

savory bake

This attractive pie has borrowed some ideas from a cheesecake!

- Serves 8
- 40 minutes
- 1 hour
- 30–35 minutes

- 2

12	slices whole-wheat (wholemeal) toast
$\frac{1}{2}$	cup (125 g) butter, cut up
$\frac{1}{4}$	cup (60 ml) cold water
$1\frac{1}{2}$	cups (400 g) ricotta cheese, drained
3	(3-ounce) packages (250 g) cream cheese, at room temperature
$\frac{1}{2}$	cup (60 g) freshly grated Parmesan cheese
3	large eggs
	Salt and freshly ground black pepper
12	cherry tomatoes, halved
	Fresh parsley, to garnish

1. **Preheat** the oven to 350°F (180°C/gas 4). Butter the bottom and sides of an 11-inch (28-cm) springform pan.

2. **Place** the toast in a food processor and chop to make fine bread crumbs.

3. **Set** aside 1 tablespoon of butter and melt the rest in a small frying pan over low heat. Add the bread crumbs and cook until the butter has been absorbed. Add the water.

4. **Firmly** press the bread crumb mixture into the bottom and sides of the prepared springform pan.

5. **Combine** the ricotta, cream cheese, Parmesan, eggs, salt, and pepper in a large bowl and beat until creamy.

6. **Spoon** over the crumb base, smoothing the surface.

7. **Arrange** the tomatoes on the top of the pie, pressing them in slightly.

8. **Bake** for 25–30 minutes, until the cheese filling is firm and browned on top.

9. **Let cool** to room temperature, at least 1 hour. Garnish with the parsley, slice, and serve.

If you liked this recipe, you will love these as well.

bubbling brussels sprouts

236

potato cakes with cherry tomatoes

252

potato bake with tomato & oregano

254

eggplant bake

Eggplant are packed with vitamins and minerals and a host of phytonutrients providing a range of health benefits, such as lowering cholesterol and preventing cancer.

Serves 6

30 minutes

1 hour

1 ½ hours

2

4	medium eggplants (aubergines), sliced ¼-inch (5-mm) thick
1	tablespoon coarse sea salt
½	cup (75 g) all-purpose (plain) flour
1	cup (250 ml) vegetable oil, for frying
2	tablespoons extra-virgin olive oil
1	small onion, finely chopped

1 ½	pounds (750 g) tomatoes, peeled and chopped
10	fresh basil leaves, torn
	Salt and freshly ground black pepper
1 ½	cups (180 g) freshly grated Parmesan cheese
8	ounces (250 g) fresh mozzarella cheese, thinly sliced

1. **Layer** the eggplant with salt in a colander. Let drain for 1 hour.

2. **Preheat** the oven to 350°F (180°C/gas 4).

3. **Rinse** the eggplants under cold running water and dry with paper towels. Dust with flour.

4. **Heat** the vegetable oil in a large frying pan over high heat. Add the eggplant in batches and fry, turning often, until golden brown. Drain on paper towels.

5. **Heat** the extra-virgin olive oil in a large frying pan over medium heat. Add the onion and sauté until softened, 3–4 minutes.

6. **Add** the tomatoes and basil, season with salt and pepper, and simmer over low heat for 20 minutes.

7. **Arrange** a layer of eggplant in an ovenproof dish. Sprinkle with Parmesan, cover with a layer of mozzarella then tomato sauce. Repeat this layering process until all the ingredients are in the dish, finishing with a layer of cheese.

8. **Bake** until golden and bubbling, about 40 minutes.

9. **Serve** hot.

If you liked this recipe, you will love these as well.

savory bake

244

zucchini lasagna
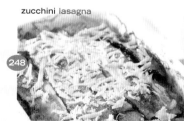
248

stuffed zucchini

256

zucchini lasagna

In this recipe we have replaced the traditional sheets of pasta with layers of thinly sliced zucchini.

Serves 4

25 minutes

45 minutes

1

½ cup (120 ml) extra-virgin olive oil

1½ pounds (750 g) zucchini (courgettes), thinly sliced lengthwise

3 cups (100 g) fresh bread crumbs

1 tablespoon butter, cut up

1 clove garlic, finely chopped

5 shallots, coarsely chopped

2 carrots, cut into small cubes

8 ounces (250 g) asparagus spears, trimmed

¾ cup (180 ml) light (single) cream

Salt

½ cup (60 g) freshly grated Parmesan cheese

1. **Preheat** the oven to 400°F (200°C/ gas 6).

2. **Heat** 5 tablespoons of oil in a large frying pan over medium heat. Add the zucchini in batches and fry until browned, about 5 minutes. Drain on paper towels.

3. **Sauté** the bread crumbs in the same pan with 2 tablespoons of oil, 1 tablespoon of butter, and the garlic, until golden, 3–4 minutes.

4. **Sauté** the shallots and carrots in the remaining oil over medium heat until browned, 3–4 minutes.

5. **Add** the asparagus and cream and simmer for 10 minutes. Season with the salt.

6. **Line** a baking dish with zucchini. Cover with a layer of asparagus mixture and sprinkle with the bread crumbs and Parmesan. Repeat until all the ingredients are in the dish, finishing with bread crumbs and Parmesan.

7. **Dot** with the remaining 1 tablespoon butter.

8. **Bake** for 15–20 minutes, until bubbling and browned on top.

9. **Serve** hot.

If you liked this recipe, you will love these as well.

eggplant bake

246

potato cakes with cherry tomatoes

252

potato bake with tomato & oregano

254

roasted vegetables
stuffed with rice

Red bell peppers are generally sweeter than yellow or green ones because they stay on the plant longer to ripen. If preferred, use a mixture of colors.

Serves 4

30 minutes

1 1/4 hours

2

2	large tomatoes
2	red or green bell peppers (capsicums)
1	cup (200 g) long-grain rice
1/3	cup (90 ml) extra-virgin olive oil
1	red onion, finely sliced
2	cloves garlic, thinly chopped
1	teaspoon dried oregano

3	tablespoons pine nuts
3	tablespoons currants
4	tablespoons finely chopped fresh basil
3	tablespoons finely chopped fresh parsley
	Salt and freshly ground black pepper

1. **Preheat** the oven to 350°F (180°C/gas 4). Oil a large baking dish.

2. **Slice** the tops off the tomatoes. Use a teaspoon to hollow them out, placing the flesh in a small bowl. Place the tomatoes upside down in a colander to drain.

3. **Cut** the tops off the bell peppers and remove the seeds and cores.

4. **Bring** a large pot of salted water to a boil. Add the rice and cook for 10 minutes. Drain and let cool in a large bowl.

5. **Heat** 2 tablespoons of oil in a large frying pan over medium heat. Add the onion, garlic, and oregano and sauté until softened, 3–4 minutes.

6. **Add** the pine nuts and currants and sauté for 2 minutes. Stir in the basil and parsley. Add this mixture and the tomato flesh to the rice. Season with salt and pepper.

7. **Stuff** the tomatoes and bell peppers with the rice.

8. **Put** in the baking dish and drizzle with the remaining oil. Bake for 50 minutes, or until tender. Serve hot.

If you liked this recipe, you will love these as well.

bell peppers with mushroom couscous

238

stuffed vegetables

242

stuffed eggplant

256

potato cakes
with cherry tomatoes

These attractive little potato cakes definitely fall under the category of comfort food! But unlike most comfort food, they are a healthy food choice.

 Serves 6

15 minutes

40–45 minutes

1

1 ½	pounds (750 g) baking (floury) potatoes, peeled and cut into chunks
½	cup (60 g) freshly grated Parmesan cheese
2	shallots, finely chopped Salt and freshly ground black pepper

4	large eggs, lightly beaten
¼	cup (60 ml) extra-virgin olive oil
1	pound (500 g) cherry tomatoes, halved
1	tablespoon finely chopped fresh thyme

1. **Preheat** the oven to 350°F (180°C/gas 4). Oil six 1-cup (250-ml) ramekins.

2. **Bring** a large pot of salted water to a boil. Add the potatoes and cook until tender, 15–20 minutes.

3. **Drain** and mash in a large bowl using a potato ricer. Add the cheese and shallots. Season with salt and pepper and mix well. Add the beaten eggs to the potato mixture and mix well.

4. **Divide** the potato mixture among the prepared ramekins, pressing it in with the back of a spoon.

5. **Bake** until lightly browned, about 20 minutes.

6. **While** the potato cakes are in the oven, heat the oil in a medium frying pan over medium heat. Add the tomatoes and thyme. Season with salt and pepper and sauté for 5 minutes. Remove from the heat.

7. **Turn** the potato cakes out onto a heated serving dish.

8. **Spoon** the tomato mixture over the top.

9. **Serve** hot.

If you liked this recipe, you will love these as well.

eggplant bake

246

zucchini lasagna

248

potato bake with tomato & oregano

254

potato bake
with tomato & oregano

If liked, grate about $\frac{1}{2}$ cup (60 g) of Parmesan cheese over the top before baking. This will add extra flavor and texture.

- Serves 4–6
- 15 minutes
- 45–50 minutes

- 1

$\frac{1}{3}$ cup (90 ml) extra-virgin olive oil

1 large onion, finely chopped

$1\frac{1}{2}$ pounds (750 g) potatoes, peeled and thinly sliced
Salt and freshly ground black pepper

12 ounces (350 g) cherry tomatoes, halved

$\frac{1}{2}$ teaspoon dried oregano or 1 teaspoon fresh oregano

$\frac{1}{2}$ cup (60 g) fine, dry bread crumbs

1. **Preheat** the oven to 400°F (200°C/gas 6). Oil a large ovenproof dish.

2. **Heat** 2 tablespoons of the oil in a large frying pan over medium heat. Add the onion and sauté until softened, 4–5 minutes.

3. **Add** the potatoes and sauté for 5 minutes. Season with salt and pepper.

4. **Transfer** to the ovenproof dish. Arrange the tomatoes in a layer on top of the potatoes. Sprinkle with oregano and bread crumbs. Drizzle with the remaining oil.

5. **Bake** until the potatoes are tender, 35–40 minutes.

6. **Serve** hot.

If you liked this recipe, you will love these as well.

tomato & zucchini gratin

240

eggplant bake

246

potato cakes with cherry tomatoes

252

stuffed eggplant

Eggplant are in season during the summer months but these roasted vegetables are light enough to serve on warm days. They are very good served at room temperature as an appetizer.

 Serves 4

🍽 20 minutes

🕐 40–45 minutes

🍸 1

4	small eggplant (aubergines)		Salt and freshly ground black pepper
8	ounces (250 g) mozzarella cheese, cut into small cubes	3	firm-ripe tomatoes, cut into small cubes
1	clove garlic, finely chopped		
2	tablespoons extra-virgin olive oil	2	tablespoons finely chopped fresh basil, to garnish

1. **Preheat** the oven to 350°F (180°C/gas 4).

2. **Cut** the eggplant in half lengthwise. Scoop out the centers and chop the flesh into small cubes.

3. **Mix** the eggplant flesh, mozzarella, and garlic in a medium bowl. Stir in the oil and season with salt and pepper.

4. **Arrange** the hollowed-out eggplant halves in an oiled baking dish. Spoon the filling mixture into the eggplants. Sprinkle with the chopped tomatoes.

5. **Bake** for 40–45 minutes, until the topping is bubbling and the eggplants are well cooked.

6. **Garnish** with the basil and serve hot or at room temperature.

If you liked this recipe, you will love these as well.

stuffed vegetables

242

roasted vegetables with rice

250

stuffed eggplant

256

eggs,
cheese
& tofu

baked tomato omelet

This recipe makes a delicious light lunch or supper. Serve with a mixed salad.

<table>
<tr><td>◎ Serves 4</td></tr>
<tr><td>🕐 15 minutes</td></tr>
<tr><td>🍳 25–30 minutes</td></tr>
<tr><td>🍴 1</td></tr>
</table>

2	tablespoons extra-virgin olive oil
1	medium onion, sliced
1	clove garlic, finely chopped
1½	teaspoons sweet paprika
1½	teaspoons ground coriander
¼	teaspoon cayenne pepper
¼	teaspoon sugar
2	(14-ounce/400-g) cans plum tomatoes, coarsely chopped, with juice
4	tablespoons finely chopped fresh parsley
	Salt and freshly ground black pepper
8	large eggs, lightly beaten
	Fresh cilantro (coriander) leaves, to garnish

1. **Heat** the oil in a medium frying pan over medium-low heat. Add the onion and garlic and sauté until softened, 3–4 minutes.

2. **Add** the paprika, coriander, cayenne, and sugar and sauté until fragrant, about 1 minute.

3. **Add** the tomatoes and cook until the sauce has thickened, about 10 minutes. Stir in the parsley and season with salt and pepper.

4. **Smooth** the sauce in pan to create an even surface. Pour the eggs over the top. Cover and cook over medium heat until set, 10–15 minutes.

5. **Serve** hot, topped with cilantro.

If you liked this recipe, you will love these as well.

tomatoes with eggs & basil

262

egg curry

266

fiery eggs with cherry tomatoes

268

tomatoes with eggs & basil

This makes enough for four starters (one stuffed tomato each) or two light lunches (or brunches).

Serves 2–4

10 minutes

15–20 minutes

4 medium-large ripe tomatoes
Salt and freshly ground black pepper
4 leaves basil, torn
4 large eggs

6 tablespoons freshly grated Parmesan cheese
2 tablespoons extra-virgin olive oil

1

1. **Preheat** the oven to 400°F (200°C/gas 6). Oil a baking dish just large enough to hold the tomatoes in a single layer.

2. **Cut** the tops off the tomatoes and use a teaspoon to hollow out the centers. Place the flesh in a bowl with the basil. Season the insides of the tomatoes lightly with salt.

3. **Break** an egg into each tomato and top up with the tomato and basil mixture. Season with salt and pepper and sprinkle with the cheese. Drizzle with the oil.

4. **Bake** for 15–20 minutes, until the tomatoes have softened and the eggs have set.

5. **Serve** hot or at room temperature.

If you liked this recipe, you will love these as well.

baked tomato omelet

260

egg curry

266

fiery eggs with cherry tomatoes

268

omelet with chinese vegetables

This recipe makes a tasty one-dish meal.

- Serves 4
- 40 minutes
- 10 minutes
- 20 minutes

- 1

2	tablespoons water	1	bok choy, coarsely chopped
2	tablespoons soy sauce	4	ounces (125 g) fresh spinach leaves, stems removed
2	teaspoons cornstarch (cornflour)		
1	teaspoon white wine	6	scallions (spring onions), sliced
4	ounces (125 g) firm tofu, coarsely chopped		
1/3	cup (90 ml) peanut oil	1	cup (250 ml) vegetable stock
2	ounces (60 g) dried bean thread or cellophane noodles, soaked in warm water for 10 minutes and drained	2	cups (100 g) mung bean sprouts
		3	large eggs, lightly beaten

1. Mix 1 tablespoon of water, 1 tablespoon of soy sauce, 1 teaspoon of cornstarch, and the white wine in a large bowl. Add the tofu and let marinate for 10 minutes.

2. Stir in 1 tablespoon of the oil. Chop the soaked noodles into short lengths. Chop the bok choy and spinach into short lengths.

3. Heat a large wok over medium heat and add 3 tablespoons of oil.

4. Add the tofu and marinade and stir-fry for 3 minutes. Remove from the wok and set aside. Add the bok choy and spinach to the wok and stir-fry for 3 minutes, or until slightly wilted.

5. Remove from the wok and set aside. Add 1 tablespoon of oil and sauté the scallions until lightly browned. Add the bean thread, vegetable stock, and remaining 1 tablespoon soy sauce.

6. Cook until the sauce has reduced, 2–3 minutes.

7. Stir in the bean sprouts. Cook for 3 more minutes. Stir in the tofu and bok choy mixtures. Transfer to a serving dish.

8. Beat the eggs with the remaining 1 tablespoon of water, and 1 teaspoon of cornstarch, in a medium bowl until frothy.

9. Heat the remaining 1 teaspoon of oil in a large frying pan over medium heat.

10. Pour in the beaten egg mixture, tilting the pan so that the batter thinly covers the bottom.

11. Cook until light golden brown on the underside, 3–5 minutes. Use a large spatula to flip the omelet and cook until golden, 2–3 minutes.

12. Serve the omelet hot with the tofu and vegetables.

egg curry

This recipe serves two as a main course or four as a starter.

Serves 2-4

20 minutes

20-25 minutes

1

- 1 tablespoon ghee (clarified butter) or vegetable oil
- 1 onion, finely chopped
- 1 (½-inch/1-cm) piece fresh ginger, thinly sliced
- 1 clove garlic, thinly sliced
- 1 teaspoon garam masala
- 1 teaspoon coriander seeds
- ½ teaspoon ground chili powder
- 1 cup (250 g) chopped tomatoes
- 1 small bunch fresh cilantro (coriander), finely chopped
- 4 hard-cooked eggs, peeled and left whole

  Freshly cooked basmati rice, to serve

1. **Heat** the ghee in a large frying pan over medium heat. Add the onion and sauté until golden brown, about 10 minutes.

2. **Add** the ginger, garlic, garam masala, coriander seeds, and ground chili and sauté for 2 minutes.

3. **Stir** in the tomatoes and cook for 5 minutes.

4. **Add** the cilantro. Add the eggs and cook over low heat until the sauce thickens, 5 minutes.

5. **Serve** hot with the rice.

If you liked this recipe, you will love these as well.

baked tomato omelet

260

tomatoes with eggs & basil

262

fiery eggs with cherry tomatoes

268

fiery eggs
with cherry tomatoes

If liked, replace the fresh cherry tomatoes in this recipe with two 14-ounce (400-g) cans of chopped tomatoes.

Serves 4

10 minutes

15 minutes

1

1/4 cup (60 ml) extra-virgin olive oil

1 onion, finely chopped

1 clove garlic, finely chopped

2 pounds (1 kg) cherry tomatoes, halved

1 fresh red or green chili, seeded and finely chopped

Salt and freshly ground black pepper

6 large eggs

Freshly baked crusty bread, to serve

1. **Heat** the oil in a large frying pan over medium heat. Add the onion and garlic and sauté until softened, about 5 minutes.

2. **Stir** in the tomatoes and chili. Season with salt and pepper.

3. **Cook** for 2 minutes.

4. **Break** the eggs into the pan. Cook until the whites are set but the yolks are still slightly runny, 5–7 minutes.

5. **Serve** hot with freshly baked bread to mop up the egg yolks and juices.

If you liked this recipe, you will love these as well.

baked tomato omelet

260

tomatoes with eggs & basil

262

egg curry

266

zucchini frittata

This versatile dish can be served for breakfast, brunch, lunch, or dinner.

- Serves 4
- 10 minutes
- 20 minutes

- 1

3	tablespoons extra-virgin olive oil
1	clove garlic, finely chopped
2	pounds (1 kg) zucchini (courgettes), thinly sliced lengthwise
	Salt and freshly ground black pepper
6	large eggs
½	cup (60 g) freshly grated pecorino or Parmesan cheese
	Fresh salad greens, to serve

1. **Heat** the oil in a large frying pan over medium heat. Add the garlic and sauté until pale gold, about 3 minutes.

2. **Add** the zucchini and sauté until tender, 5–7 minutes. Season with salt and pepper.

3. **Beat** the eggs and cheese in a medium bowl.

4. **Pour** the egg mixture into the pan and cook until the egg is almost solid, 7–8 minutes.

5. **Slide** the frittata onto a plate, flip it onto another plate, and then slide it back into the pan. Cook until golden brown and the egg is cooked through, 3–4 minutes.

6. **Serve** hot.

If you liked this recipe, you will love these as well.

omelet with chinese vegetables

264

basil frittata

272

cheese soufflé

274

basil frittata

Replace the basil with the same amount of chopped fresh parsley or cilantro (coriander) for an equally delicious frittata.

- Serves 6
- 10 minutes
- 10 minutes

- 2

12	large eggs
1	cup (120 g) freshly grated pecorino or Parmesan cheese
	Salt and freshly ground black pepper

Bunch of fresh basil leaves, coarsely chopped + extra leaves, to garnish

2 tablespoons extra-virgin olive oil

1. **Beat** the eggs in a large bowl. Add the cheese and season with salt and pepper. Add the basil and mix well.

2. **Heat** the oil in a large frying pan over medium heat. Pour the egg mixture into the pan and cook until the bottom is browned, 3–5 minutes.

3. **Slide** the frittata onto a plate, flip it onto another plate, and then slide it back into the pan. Cook until the egg is cooked through and lightly browned all over, 3–4 minutes.

4. **Transfer** to a serving dish. Garnish with basil, and serve hot.

If you liked this recipe, you will love these as well.

baked tomato omelet

260

omelet with chinese vegetables

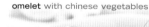

264

zucchini frittata

274

cheese soufflé

You could also bake this in a single 4-cup (1-liter) soufflé dish. If you do, add 5–10 minutes to the baking time.

Serves 4

10 minutes

25–30 minutes

2

4	large eggs, separated	4	ounces (120 g) Cheddar or
1¼	cups (300 ml) milk, warmed		Emmental cheese, grated
1	tablespoon butter, melted		Salt and freshly ground
1	teaspoon Dijon mustard		black pepper
3	cups (100 g) fresh bread crumbs		

1. **Preheat** the oven to 350°F (180°C/gas 4). Butter four 1-cup (250-ml) ramekins or soufflé dishes.

2. **Lightly** beat the egg yolks in a large bowl.

3. **Add** the milk, butter, and mustard to the egg yolks and mix well.

4. **Stir** in the bread crumbs and cheese and season with the salt and pepper.

5. **Beat** the egg whites with a pinch of salt until stiff peaks form. Fold into the yolk mixture.

6. **Pour** into the prepared dishes. Bake for 25–30 minutes, until well risen, brown on top, and set in the middle.

7. **Serve** at once.

If you liked this recipe, you will love these as well.

tomatoes with eggs & basil

262

basil frittata

272

zucchini frittata

270

tofu with mushrooms

Tofu, also known as bean curd, is made by coagulating soy milk and then pressing the resulting curds into soft white blocks. It was invented in China more than 2,000 years ago.

Serves 6

20 minutes

25 minutes

1

	Vegetable oil, for frying
2	pounds (1 kg) firm tofu, cubed
3	tablespoons peanut oil
2	scallions (spring onions), thinly sliced
1	tablespoon finely chopped fresh ginger
1	pound (500 g) button mushrooms, sliced
½	cup (120 g) thinly sliced bamboo shoots

1	cup (250 ml) vegetable stock
2½	tablespoons soy sauce
1	teaspoon Asian sesame oil Freshly ground black pepper
4	baby bok choy, cut in half
2	teaspoons cornstarch (cornflour)
1	tablespoon water

1. **Place** a wok over high heat. Pour in about 2 inches (5 cm) of oil. Test the oil temperature by dropping in a small piece of bread. If it immediately bubbles to the surface and begins to turn golden, the oil is ready.

2. **Add** the tofu in two batches and fry until golden brown all over, 5–7 minutes per batch.

3. **Drain** on paper towels.

4. **Heat** the peanut oil in a wok, add the scallions and ginger and stir-fry until softened, 2–3 minutes.

5. **Add** the mushrooms and stir-fry for 3 minutes.

6. **Stir** in the bamboo shoots, vegetable stock, soy sauce, sesame oil, and the fried tofu. Season with pepper. Bring to a boil and simmer for 3 minutes.

7. **Add** the bok choy and cook for 2 minutes more.

8. **Mix** the cornstarch and water in a small bowl. Stir into the wok and cook to thicken the mixture, 1–2 minutes.

9. **Serve** hot.

If you liked this recipe, you will love these as well.

tofu & black bean stir-fry

278

spicy tofu

280

tempeh stir-fry

282

tofu & black bean stir-fry

Kecap manis is a dark brown, fairly sweet Indonesian soy sauce. It is available in Asian supermarkets; if you can't find it replace with sweet, dark soy sauce.

Serves 4

15 minutes

10 minutes

1

2	tablespoons Asian sesame oil
1	medium onion, sliced
2	cloves garlic, sliced
2	tablespoons Chinese fermented black beans, chopped
2	large fresh red chilies, seeded and sliced
1	teaspoon finely chopped fresh ginger
12	ounces (350 g) firm tofu, sliced

2	tablespoons light soy sauce
2	tablespoons kecap manis or sweet soy sauce
1	bunch Chinese broccoli, or regular broccoli, in florets
5	ounces (150 g) oyster or shiitake mushrooms, halved
1	red bell pepper (capsicum), seeded and sliced
½	Chinese cabbage (wom bok), chopped
	Freshly cooked jasmine rice, to serve

1. **Heat** the oil in a large wok over medium-high heat. Add the onion, garlic, black beans, chiles, and ginger and stir-fry until softened, 2–3 minutes.

2. **Add** the tofu and stir-fry until golden brown, 2 minutes.

3. **Pour** in the soy sauce and kecap manis and toss to coat. Add the broccoli and cook for 1 minute.

4. **Add** the mushrooms and bell pepper and stir-fry until vegetables are slightly tender but still crisp, about 2 more minutes.

5. **Stir** in the Chinese cabbage and stir-fry until wilted, about 1 minute.

6. **Serve** hot with jasmine rice.

If you liked this recipe, you will love these as well.

tofu with mushrooms

276

spicy tofu

280

tempeh stir-fry

282

spicy tofu

Tofu is a good source of lean plant protein and regular consumption is believed to help lower cholesterol levels.

Serves 6

20 minutes

15 minutes

10 minutes

1

2	teaspoons dried black mushrooms
2	stalks celery, finely chopped
2	cloves garlic, finely chopped
2	tablespoons vegetable oil
2	pounds (1 kg) firm tofu, cubed
2	fresh red chilies, chopped
1½	cups (375 ml) vegetable stock
1	tablespoon soy sauce

1	tablespoon Asian sesame oil
½	teaspoon sugar
1	tablespoon water
1	teaspoon cornstarch (cornflour)
	Freshly ground black pepper
1	tablespoon finely chopped fresh parsley

1. **Soak** the dried mushrooms in ¼ cup (60 ml) warm water for 15 minutes.

2. **Sauté** the celery and garlic in the vegetable oil in a large wok over medium heat for 3 minutes.

3. **Add** the mushrooms, tofu, and chilies and stir-fry for 3 minutes.

4. **Stir** in the vegetable stock, soy sauce, sesame oil, and sugar. Stir-fry for 5 minutes, or until the liquid has reduced slightly.

5. **Mix** the water and cornstarch in a small bowl. Stir into the wok to thicken the sauce.

6. **Season** with pepper, garnish with the parsley, and serve hot.

If you liked this recipe, you will love these as well.

tofu with mushrooms

276

tofu & black bean stir-fry

278

tempeh stir-fry

282

tempeh stir-fry

Tempeh is a soy product from Indonesia. It is made by a natural culturing and fermentation process that binds soybeans into a cake form. Tempeh has a firm texture and an earthy flavor which becomes more pronounced as it ages. Because of its high nutritional value, tempeh is widely used in vegetarian cuisine.

- Serves 4
- 30 minutes
- 10 minutes

- 1

¼	cup (60 ml) vegetable oil
10	ounces (300 g) tempeh, thinly sliced
2	tablespoons Asian sesame oil
1	onion, sliced
2	cloves garlic, sliced
1	(¾-inch/2-cm) piece fresh ginger, peeled and finely chopped
2	fresh red chilies, seeded and finely chopped
1	small head broccoli, cut into florets
8	ounces (250 g) green beans, trimmed and cut into short lengths
1	red bell pepper (capsicum), seeded and thinly sliced
1	green bell pepper (capsicum), seeded and thinly sliced
½	cup (120 ml) Thai satay or peanut sauce
2	tablespoons soy sauce
1	cup (50 g) mung bean sprouts
	Jasmine rice, to serve

1. **Heat** the vegetable oil in a large wok over medium-high heat. Add the tempeh and stir-fry until crisp, 2–3 minutes. Remove using a slotted spoon and set aside to drain on paper towels. Discard any remaining oil.

2. **Heat** the sesame oil in the wok over medium heat. Add the onion, garlic, ginger, and chile and stir-fry until softened, about 5 minutes.

3. **Add** the broccoli and green beans and stir-fry for 2 minutes. Add the red and green bell peppers and stir-fry until vegetables are slightly tender but still crisp, 2–3 more minutes. Pour in the satay sauce and soy sauce and heat through. Toss to coat.

4. **Serve** with jasmine rice and topped with bean sprouts.

If you liked this recipe, you will love these as well.

stir-fried vegetables with noodles

206

tofu with mushrooms

276

tofu & black bean stir-fry

278

savory tarts & focaccia

onion tarte tatins

Serve these exquisite little onion tarts with a green or mixed salad for lunch.

- Serves 4
- 20 minutes
- 10 minutes
- 45–60 minutes

- 2

¼ cup (60 g) butter
+ 1–2 tablespoons extra
for the pan

3 large white onions, sliced
into wedges about ⅔ inch
(1.5 cm) thick

3 large red onions, sliced
into wedges about ⅔ inch
(1.5 cm) thick

1 tablespoon honey

1 tablespoon brined green
peppercorns, drained

1 tablespoon pine nuts

5 tablespoon freshly grated
Parmesan cheese

Salt and freshly ground
black pepper

1 (12-ounce/350-g) sheet
ready-rolled puff pastry

1. **Melt** ¼ cup (60 g) butter in a large frying pan over low heat. Add the onions, cover, and sweat until soft, 20–30 minutes. Stir often.

2. **Uncover**, add the honey, and increase the heat, stirring constantly, until the onions are caramelized and the juice reduces to a sticky glaze. Stir in the peppercorns, pine nuts, and 3 tablespoons of Parmesan. Season with salt and pepper.

3. **Preheat** the oven to 375°F (190°C/gas 5). Brush four 4-inch (10-cm) tartlet pans with melted butter. Sprinkle with the remaining 2 tablespoons of Parmesan.

4. **Spoon** the onions into the tartlet pans, spreading evenly.

5. **Cut** the pastry into four 5-inch (12-cm) rounds. Place over the onions, press down gently, and tuck in the edges between the onions and the pans.

6. **Bake** for 25–30 minutes, until golden brown.

7. **Let** cool for 10 minutes, then run a knife around the edges. Place a plate on top and turn the tartlets out. Serve warm.

If you liked this recipe, you will love these as well.

leek tartlets

288

mushroom & herb tart

298

filled onion focaccia

308

leek tartlets

Just use the white and pale green bottom parts of the leeks.

 Serves 4–6

15 minutes

45 minutes

1

3 tablespoons extra-virgin olive oil

3 medium leeks, trimmed, cleaned, and coarsely chopped

2 celery stalks, trimmed and coarsely chopped

1¼ cups (300 ml) heavy (double) cream

½ cup (25 g) coarsely chopped fresh parsley, leaves only

1 (12-ounce/350-g) sheet ready-rolled puff pastry

1 large egg, lightly beaten
Salt and freshly ground black pepper

1. **Preheat** the oven to 375°F (190°C/gas 5).

2. **Brush** a baking sheet with melted butter.

3. **Heat** the oil in a large frying pan over medium-low heat, add the leeks, and sauté until the leeks are tender but not browned, about 8–10 minutes.

4. **Add** the celery and cream, and simmer until the celery has softened, about 5 minutes.

5. **Stir** in the parsley and set aside.

6. **Unroll** the pastry and cut into four to six squares. Place on the baking sheet

7. **Mix** the egg into the slightly cooled leek mixture and season with salt and plenty of pepper.

8. **Top** the pieces of pastry with the leek mixture. Leave a ¾-inch (1.5-cm) border all around.

9. **Bake** for 30 minutes, until set and golden in places. Serve warm.

If you liked this recipe, you will love these as well.

onion tarte tatins

286

macedonian spinach pie

300

filled onion focaccia

308

herb & blue cheese turnovers

These hearty turnovers make a perfect lunch dish. If you can't get crème fraîche, replace it with sour cream.

Serves 4

20–30 minutes

30 minutes

45–50 minutes

2

PASTRY

3	cups (450 g) all-purpose (plain) flour
1	teaspoon salt
1/2	cup (120 g) unsalted butter, chilled and diced
3	tablespoons finely chopped fresh parsley
1	tablespoon finely chopped fresh tarragon
1	large egg yolk
2	tablespoons iced water + 2–3 tablespoons, if needed

FILLING

1	pound (500 g) potatoes, peeled and diced
4	scallions (spring onions), finely chopped
3	tablespoons finely chopped fresh parsley
3	tablespoons finely chopped watercress
4	ounces hard blue cheese
1	hard-boiled egg chopped
2	tablespoons crème fraîche
1	large egg, separated
	Salt and freshly ground black pepper

1. **To prepare the pastry,** combine the flour and salt in a large bowl. Cut in the butter with a pastry blender, or pulse the mixture in a food processor, until it resembles fine bread crumbs.

2. **Mix** the herbs, egg yolk, and water in a food processor or blender. Add the herb mixture to the flour mixture.

3. **Knead** or pulse, adding enough additional water (2–3 tablespoons) to obtain a smooth, firm dough.

4. **Press** into a log, wrap in plastic wrap (cling film), and chill in the refrigerator for at least 30 minutes.

5. **To prepare the filling,** mix the potatoes with scallions, parsley, and watercress in a bowl. Stir in the cheese and hard-boiled egg.

6. **Whisk** the crème fraîche with the egg yolk in a small bowl, reserving the white. Stir the crème fraîche mixture into the potato mixture. Season well with salt and pepper and set aside.

7. **Preheat** the oven to 350°F (180°C/ gas 4). Line a large baking sheet with parchment paper.

8. **Unwrap** the pastry and divide into four equal pieces. Flour a work surface and roll out each piece into a circle, 8–9 inches (20–22 cm) in diameter. Use a plate as a guide and cut around.

9. **Divide** the filling evenly among the dough circles, spooning a quarter onto one-half of each and leaving a border around the edge. Brush the edges with egg white, or moisten with water, and fold the dough over the filling. Crimp the edges together. Prick each turnover with a fork and brush with the remaining egg white.

10. **Use** a spatula to transfer the turnovers to the baking sheet.

11. **Bake** for 45–50 minutes, until the turnovers are golden and the filling is cooked. Serve hot.

goat cheese turnovers

These goat cheese turnovers make an elegant starter for eight. Serve with a small mixed green salad of arugula (rocket) or radicchio.

Serves 8

30 minutes

1 hour

10–15 minutes

1

1⅔ cups (250 g) all-purpose (plain) flour

⅓ cup (90 ml) extra-virgin olive oil

⅓ cup (90 ml) water + 2 tablespoons

5 ounces (150 g) chèvre or other soft fresh goat cheese

2 tablespoons finely chopped fresh thyme

Salt and freshly ground black pepper

1 large egg white

1. **Sift** the flour into a large bowl. Add half the oil and ⅓ cup (90 ml) water. Mix to a smooth dough. Shape into a ball and wrap in plastic wrap (cling film). Chill in the refrigerator for 1 hour. Stir the goat cheese in a small bowl until smooth.

2. **Add** half the thyme. Season with salt and pepper.

3. **Preheat** the oven to 400°F (200°C/gas 6). Oil a large baking sheet.

4. **Divide** the dough into eight pieces. Roll out on a floured work surface into ⅛-inch (3-mm)-thick circles. Spoon the cheese mixture onto one-half each circle. Beat the egg white and remaining 2 tablespoons water in a small bowl and brush the edges of the pastry. Fold over the filling. Pinch the edges together to seal.

5. **Place** on the sheet. Brush with some of the remaining oil.

6. **Bake** for 5 minutes. Brush with the remaining oil. Bake until puffed and golden brown, 5–10 minutes.

7. **Serve** hot.

If you liked this recipe, you will love these as well.

herb & blue cheese turnovers

290

spinach & ricotta turnovers

294

filled focaccia with gorgonzola & bell peppers

310

spinach & ricotta turnovers

Serve these delicious turnovers warm. They are quite hearty and are a meal in themselves.

⊚ Serves 4

🍽 45 minutes

🌡 2¼ hours

🍴 30–35 minutes

🍸 2

DOUGH

1⅔ cups (250 g) all-purpose (plain) flour

½ teaspoon salt

¼ cup (60 g) unsalted butter, cut into cubes and softened

2 tablespoons freshly grated Parmesan cheese

½ cup (125 ml) milk, warmed (110°F/43°C)

½ ounce (15 g) fresh yeast, or 1 (¼ ounce/ 7-g) package active dry yeast

1 teaspoon dark brown sugar

1 small egg, beaten, to glaze

FILLING

2 tablespoons extra-virgin olive oil

2 scallions (spring onions), trimmed and sliced

1 clove garlic, sliced

½ teaspoon red pepper flakes

8 ounces (250 g) white mushrooms, sliced

1 pound (500 g) fresh spinach

8 ounces (250 g) ricotta cheese

1 large egg, lightly beaten

Salt and freshly ground black pepper

1. **To prepare the dough,** mix the flour and salt in a large bowl. Rub in the butter and cheese until the mixture resemble coarse crumbs.

2. **Stir** the milk, yeast, and brown sugar in a separate bowl until dissolved. Set aside until frothy, 10–15 minutes.

3. **Add** the yeast mixture to the flour and mix with a fork to form a soft, sticky dough. Cover with plastic wrap (cling film) and let rest for 15 minutes.

4. **Lightly** oil your hands and gently knead the dough for 10 seconds. Cover the bowl again, and repeat these periods of resting and brief kneading twice more. Then let the dough rise for 1 hour in a warm place.

5. **To prepare the filling,** heat the oil in a medium pan over medium heat. Add the scallions, garlic, crushed red pepper, and mushrooms and sauté until slightly colored, about 5 minutes.

6. **Put** the spinach in a colander and pour boiling water over to wilt the leaves.

Press out as much liquid as possible.

7. **Beat** the ricotta and egg in a large bowl and season with salt and a good grinding of pepper. Stir in the mushroom mixture and the spinach. Lightly flour a work surface, place the dough on it, knead briefly with floured hands, then divide into four pieces.

8. **Roll** out each piece into a circle, about 8 inches (20 cm) in diameter. Spoon a quarter of the filling onto one-half of each circle. Moisten the edges with a little water, fold over, and crimp the edges to seal. Line a baking sheet with parchment paper.

9. **Place** the turnovers on the sheet and let rise for 30 minutes.

10. **Preheat** the oven to 400°F (200°C/gas 6).

11. **Brush** the turnovers with the egg glaze and cut 3 diagonal slits with a sharp knife in the top of each. Bake for 30–35 minutes, until golden and crisp. Serve warm.

swiss chard & walnut tart

This tart makes a delicious lunch dish. Serve with a mixed salad.

Serves 6

30 minutes

30 mnutes

50 minutes

2

PASTRY

1⅔ cups (250 g) all-purpose (plain) flour

Pinch of salt

¼ cup (30 g) finely grated Parmesan cheese

1 large egg, beaten

5 tablespoons (75 ml) extra-virgin olive oil

¼ cup (60 ml) warm water

FILLING

¼ cup (60 g) unsalted butter

2 medium onions, finely sliced

8 ounces (250 g) Swiss chard, leaves and stems separated and thinly sliced

1½ cups (150 g) walnuts, coarsely chopped

Salt and freshly ground black pepper

2 large eggs + 1 large egg yolk

1 cup (250 ml) crème fraîche or sour cream

½ cup (60 g) freshly grated Gruyère cheese

1. **To prepare the pastry,** combine the flour, salt, and Parmesan in a bowl. Add the egg, oil, and enough water to form a smooth dough. Knead briefly on a lightly floured work surface. Form into a ball, wrap in plastic wrap (cling film), and refrigerate for 30 minutes.

2. **Preheat** the oven to 400°F (200°C/ gas 6).

3. **Unwrap** the pastry and roll out into an 11-inch (28-cm) circle. Loosely wrap around the rolling pin and unroll over a 9-inch (23-cm) tart pan with a removable bottom. Gently press into the pan to line the bottom and sides. Prick all over with a fork, line with parchment paper, and fill with pie weights or dried beans.

4. **Bake** for 10 minutes, until the edges are just golden. Remove the paper and beans and bake for 5 more minutes. Remove from the oven and set aside.

5. **To prepare the filling,** decrease the oven temperature to 350°F (180°C/gas 4).

6. **Melt** the butter in a large frying pan over medium heat. Add the onions and sauté until softened, 3–4 minutes. Add the chard stems and walnuts. Sauté until the stems begin to soften, 2–3 minutes. Mix in the chard leaves and cook until wilted, 1–2 minutes. Season to taste with salt and pepper. With a slotted spoon, transfer the chard mixture into the pastry shell, discarding any juice.

7. **Whisk** together the eggs, egg yolk, and crème fraîche in a bowl. Stir in the cheese and pour over the chard filling, making sure it oozes down through the filling.

8. **Bake** for 25 minutes, until golden and set. Serve hot or at room temperature.

mushroom & herb tart

Serve this special pie warm with a green salad and some fresh creamy cheese.

- Serves 6
- 25 minutes
- 1 hour
- 25–30 minutes

- 2

1	recipe shortcrust pastry (see page 296)

FILLING

3	tablespoons extra-virgin olive oil
1	onion, finely chopped
2	cloves garlic, crushed
8	ounces (250 g) porcini or cremini mushrooms, sliced
½	cup finely chopped parsley
½	cup snipped fresh chives
2	tablespoons finely chopped fresh thyme
1	large egg + 1 large egg yolk
¾	cup (200 ml) crème fraîche or heavy (double) cream
	Salt and freshly ground black pepper
½	cup (50 g) grated Gruyère cheese

1. **Prepare** the pastry and bake blind following the instructions on page 296. Set aside.
2. **To prepare the filling,** heat the oil in a large frying pan over medium heat. Add the onion and garlic and sauté until softened, 3–4 minutes.
3. **Add** the mushrooms and sauté for 2 minutes.
4. **Remove** from the heat and stir in the herbs. Set aside.
5. **Whisk** the egg and egg yolk in a bowl and beat in the crème fraîche. Season with salt and pepper and combine with the mushroom mixture.
6. **Spoon** the filling into the tart shell and sprinkle with the Gruyère cheese.
7. **Bake** for 20–25 minutes, until golden brown.
8. **Serve** warm or at room temperature.

If you liked this recipe, you will love these as well.

swiss chard & walnut tart

296

macedonian spinach pie

300

herb & tomato focaccia

306

macedonian spinach pie

As the name suggests, this dish comes from the Balkans. If liked, use filo (phyllo) pastry instead of puff pastry. Serve the pie warm, with a bowl of plain Greek-style yogurt.

Serves 6

45 minutes

40–45 minutes

2

- 2 pounds (1 kg) fresh spinach
- 2 tablespoons extra-virgin olive oil
- 1 white onion, finely chopped
- 2 cloves garlic, thinly sliced
- 3 tablespoons finely chopped fresh thyme
- 1 tablespoon finely chopped fresh oregano
- 2 sage leaves, chopped
  Salt and freshly ground black pepper
- Grating of nutmeg
- 5 ounces (150 g) soft goat cheese or feta cheese, diced
- 2 (9$\frac{1}{4}$ x 9$\frac{1}{2}$-inch/24 x 24-cm) sheets ready-rolled puff pastry
- 1 tablespoon fresh bread crumbs
- 5 small eggs

1. **Steam** the spinach until wilted, 1–2 minutes. Drain and chop finely. Squeeze out excess moisture.

2. **Heat** the oil in a frying pan over medium heat. Add the onion and sauté until softened, 3–4 minutes. Remove from the heat, and add the spinach, garlic, and herbs. Season with salt, pepper, and nutmeg. Stir in the cheese.

3. **Oil** a 9-inch (23-cm) springform pan.

4. **Roll** a pastry sheet out thinly. Cut out an 11-inch (28-cm) circle. Line the bottom and sides with the pastry.

5. **Sprinkle** with bread crumbs and

spoon in the filling.

6. **Make** four hollows in the filling and break an egg into each.

7. **Cut** a 9-inch (23-cm) circle from the remaining pastry. Place on the pie. Cut two small holes in the center to let steam escape.

8. **Beat** the remaining egg and brush the pie with it. Sprinkle with sesame seeds.

9. **Preheat** the oven to 400°F (200°C/gas 6).

10. **Bake** for 30–35 minutes, until puffed and golden brown.

11. **Serve** hot.

If you liked this recipe, you will love these as well.

spinach & ricotta turnovers

294

swiss chard & walnut tart

296

mushroom & herb tart

298

focaccia with sage & olives

Focaccia is a type of Italian flatbread. It can be plain with just a little sea salt and olive oil sprinkled over the top, or can include toppings and fillings. You can also knead herbs and other flavorings into the dough itself. Once you have the basic method, feel free to experiment.

Serves 6–8

30 minutes

1½ hours

20–25 minutes

2

BASIC FOCACCIA DOUGH

1   ounce (30 g) fresh yeast or 2 (¼-ounce/7-g) packages active dry yeast
1   teaspoon sugar
1½ cups (350 ml) warm water
3⅓ cups (500 g) all-purpose (plain) flour
1   teaspoon salt
¼   cup (60 ml) extra-virgin olive oil

TOPPING

12 sage leaves, finely chopped
½   cup (50 g) pitted black olives, coarsely chopped
2   tablespoons extra-virgin olive oil

1. **To prepare the dough,** combine the yeast and sugar in a small bowl. Add half the warm water and stir with a fork until the yeast has dissolved. Set aside until frothy, 10–15 minutes.

2. **Put** the flour and salt in a large bowl. Pour in the yeast mixture, most of the remaining water, and the oil. Stir until the flour is absorbed, adding more water as required. Now it is ready to knead.

3. **Transfer** the dough to a floured work surface and shape into a compact ball. Press down on the dough with your knuckles to spread it. Take the far end of the dough, fold it a short distance toward you, then push it away again with the heel of your palm. Flexing your wrist, fold it toward you again, give it a quarter turn, then push it away. Repeat, gently and with the lightest possible touch, for 8–10 minutes, until the dough is smooth and elastic, shows definite air bubbles beneath the surface, and springs back if you flatten it with your palm.

4. **Put** in a large oiled bowl and cover with a cloth. Set aside until doubled in bulk, about 1½ hours. To test, poke your finger gently into the dough; if the impression remains, it is ready.

5. **Preheat** the oven to 425°F (220°C/gas 7).

6. **Transfer** the dough to a lightly floured work surface and knead for 2–3 minutes.

7. **Place** the dough on a large oiled baking sheet and, using your hands, spread into a circle about 12 inches (30 cm) in diameter and ½ inch (1 cm) thick. Dimple the surface with your fingertips.

8. **To prepare the topping,** sprinkle with the sage and olives and drizzle with the oil.

9. **Bake** until pale golden brown, 20–25 minutes. Serve hot or at room temperature.

potato focaccia with cherry tomatoes & oregano

Serve this focaccia warm with a soup or salad.

- Serves 6–8
- 25 minutes
- 2½ hours
- 35–40 minutes
- 2

1	large baking (floury) potato, peeled and cut into small cubes
1	recipe basic focaccia dough (see page 302)
20	cherry tomatoes, halved
1	teaspoon coarse sea salt
1	tablespoon finely chopped fresh oregano
2	tablespoons extra-virgin olive oil

1. **Cook** the potato in a small pot of salted boiling water until tender, about 10 minutes. Drain and mash until smooth.

2. **Prepare** the focaccia dough, up to the point where it is ready to knead. Gradually work the mashed potato into the dough as you knead. Let rise in a warm place until doubled in bulk, about 2 hours.

3. **Oil** a 10-inch (25-cm) round baking pan and press the dough onto the baking pan using your fingers. Sprinkle with the tomatoes, coarse salt, and oregano.

4. **Drizzle** with the oil and let rise for 30 minutes.

5. **Preheat** the oven to 425°F (220°C/ gas 7). Bake until the focaccia is golden brown, 25–30 minutes.

6. **Serve** hot or at room temperature.

If you liked this recipe, you will love these as well.

focaccia with sage & olives

302

herb & tomato focaccia

306

filled focaccia with gorgonzola & bell peppers

310

herb & tomato focaccia

If liked, add 5 ounces (150 g) of coarsely grated or chopped mozzarella cheese to the topping just before baking.

- ⊚ Serves 6–8
- 🕐 25 minutes
- 🕐 2 hours
- 🕐 20–25 minutes

- 🍸 2

1	recipe basic focaccia dough (see page 302)
6	tablespoons extra-virgin olive oil
1	medium onion, very finely chopped
2	cloves garlic, very finely chopped
3	tablespoons finely chopped fresh parsley
2	tablespoons finely chopped fresh basil
1	tablespoon finely chopped fresh rosemary
½	teaspoon dried oregano Freshly ground black pepper
1	(14-ounce/400-g) can tomatoes, with juice, chopped Salt

1. **Prepare** the focaccia dough up to the point where the dough is ready to knead. Gradually work 2 tablespoons of the oil into the dough as you knead. Let rise in a warm place until doubled in bulk, about 2 hours.

2. **Preheat** the oven to 450°F (250°C/gas 8). Lightly oil a large baking sheet.

3. **Turn** the dough out onto a lightly floured work surface and knead for 5 minutes. Spread out into a large oval on the prepared sheet.

4. **Mix** the onion, garlic, parsley, basil, rosemary, and oregano in a small bowl. Add 2 tablespoons of the remaining oil and season with pepper. Spread the tomatoes over the focaccia and top with the herb mixture. Season with salt, and drizzle with the remaining oil.

5. **Bake** until the focaccia is golden brown, 20–25 minutes.

6. **Serve** hot or at room temperature.

If you liked this recipe, you will love these as well.

focaccia with sage & olives

302

potato focaccia with cherry tomatoes & oregano

304

baby focaccias with olives & pine nuts

312

filled onion focaccia

The longer you cook the onions over very low heat the more delicious this bread will be. Let them caramelize and melt into a sweet mush if you have the time.

Serves 6–8

35 minutes

1½ hours

About 1 hour

2

| 1 | recipe basic focaccia dough (see page 302) |
| ¼ | cup (60 ml) extra-virgin olive oil |

| 4 | large white onions, thinly sliced |
| | Salt |

1. **Prepare** the focaccia dough and let rise in a warm place until doubled in bulk, about 1½ hours.

2. **Preheat** the oven to 425°F (220°C/gas 7). Oil a 12-inch (30-cm) pizza pan. Heat the oil in a large frying pan. Add the onions and simmer on low heat until tender and beginning to caramelize, about 40 minutes. Season lightly with salt.

3. **Turn** the dough out onto a lightly floured work surface and knead for 5 minutes. Divide into two equal portions.

4. **Roll** out each piece of dough into a 12-inch (30-cm) circle. Line the prepared pan with one piece of dough. Spread with the onions. Cover with the remaining dough.

5. **Bake** until golden brown, 20–25 minutes.

6. **Serve** hot or at room temperature.

If you liked this recipe, you will love these as well.

onion tarte tatins

286

leek tartlets

288

filled focaccia with gorgonzola & bell peppers

310

filled focaccia with gorgonzola & bell peppers

Gorgonzola is an Italian blue cheese. If preferred, you can replace it in this recipe with another blue cheese, such as Danish blue, Roquefort, or Stilton.

Serves 6–8

45 minutes

1½ hours

55–60 minutes

2

1	recipe basic focaccia dough (see page 302)
1	large red bell pepper (capsicum)
1	large yellow pepper (capsicum)
1	clove garlic, thinly sliced
8	ounces (250 g) Gorgonzola cheese, sliced

Salt and freshly ground black pepper

4	tablespoons (60 ml) extra-virgin olive oil
12	cherry tomatoes
1	teaspoon dried oregano

1. **Prepare** the dough and let rise in a warm place until doubled in bulk, about 1½ hours.

2. **Preheat** the oven to 400°F (200°C gas 6). Oil a 9 x 13-inch (23 x 33-cm) baking pan.

3. **Bake** the bell peppers for 20–30 minutes, until charred all over. Put in a plastic bag and let rest for 10 minutes. Peel and seed, then slice thinly.

4. **Turn** the dough out onto a floured surface and knead for 5 minutes.

5. **Divide** in two and press one into the prepared pan.

6. **Cover** with the peppers, garlic, and Gorgonzola. Season with salt and pepper and drizzle with 2 tablespoons of oil.

7. **Roll** out the remaining dough into a rectangle large enough to cover the pan. Cover the filling with the dough.

8. **Press** the cherry tomatoes into the top at regular intervals. Sprinkle with oregano and drizzle with the remaining 2 tablespoons oil.

9. **Bake** for 25–30 minutes, until golden brown. Serve warm.

If you liked this recipe, you will love these as well.

potato focaccia with cherry tomatoes & oregano
304

filled onion focaccia
308

focaccia filled with zucchini & basmati rice
314

baby focaccias
with olives & pine nuts

Serve these versatile little savories as a snack or as part of a party spread.

- ⊚ Serves 6–8
- ⊚ 35 minutes
- ⊚ 1½ hours
- ⊚ 35–45 minutes

- ⊚ 2

1	recipe basic focaccia dough (see page 302)
1	small green bell pepper (capsicum)
1	small yellow bell pepper (capsicum)
1	small red bell pepper (capsicum)
3	tablespoons black olive paste or tapenade
16	black olives, pitted and coarsely chopped
2	tablespoons pine nuts
	Salt and freshly ground black pepper
2	tablespoons extra-virgin olive oil

1. **Prepare** the dough and let rise in a warm place until doubled in bulk, about 1½ hours.

2. **Preheat** the oven to 425°F (220°C/gas 7). Bake the bell peppers for 20–30 minutes, until charred all over.

3. **Place** in a plastic bag and let rest for 10 minutes. Peel and seed, then slice thinly. Oil two large baking sheets.

4. **Turn** the dough out onto a lightly floured work surface and knead for 5 minutes, adding the olive paste as you work.

5. **Divide** the dough into 16 equal portions and press into rounds about ½ inch (1 cm) thick. Place on the prepared baking sheets.

6. **Top** each round with some of the peppers, olives, and pine nuts. Season with salt and pepper. Drizzle with the oil.

7. **Bake** until golden brown, about 15 minutes.

8. **Serve** warm.

If you liked this recipe, you will love these as well.

focaccia with sage & olives

302

potato focaccia with cherry tomatoes & oregano

304

filled focaccia with gorgonzola & bell peppers

310

focaccia filled
with zucchini & basmati rice

Serve slices of this hearty filled loaf with a mixed salad for lunch.

- Serves 6–8
- 30 minutes
- 2 hours
- 50–55 minutes
- 2

1	recipe basic focaccia dough (see page 302)
4	tablespoons (60 ml) extra-virgin olive oil
4	medium zucchini (courgettes), coarsely grated
1	clove garlic, finely chopped

	Salt
½	cup (100 g) basmati rice
1	large egg, lightly beaten
2	tablespoons finely chopped fresh cilantro (coriander)
2	tablespoons sesame seeds

1. **Prepare** the dough up to the point where it is ready to knead. Gradually work in 1 tablespoon of oil. Let rise until doubled in bulk, about 2 hours.

2. **Heat** 2 tablespoons of oil in a large frying pan over medium heat. Add the zucchini and garlic and sauté until tender, 7–10 minutes. Season with salt.

3. **Cook** the rice in salted boiling water until tender, 12–15 minutes. Drain and stir into the zucchini mixture.

4. **Let** cool slightly. Add the egg and cilantro. Mix well.

5. **Preheat** the oven to 400°F (200°C/ gas 6) Oil a large baking sheet. Turn the dough out onto a floured surface and knead for 5 minutes.

6. **Roll** into a circle about 15 inches (40 cm) in diameter. Place on the baking sheet.

7. **Place** the zucchini mixture in the center and pull the edges over the top.

8. **Brush** with the remaining oil and sprinkle with the sesame seeds.

9. **Bake** for 30–35 minutes, until golden.

10. **Serve** hot.

If you liked this recipe, you will love these as well.

potato focaccia with cherry tomatoes & oregano

304

filled onion focaccia

308

filled focaccia with gorgonzola & bell peppers

310

Index